LUTHERAN HIGH SCHOOL RELIGION SERIES

The Last Word

Hebrews, the General Epistles, and the Revelation of St. John

Teachers Guide

By Robert M. Carpenter and Dale E. Griffin
Edited by the Board for Parish Services Staff

CONCORDIA PUBLISHING HOUSE
3558 SOUTH JEFFERSON AVENUE
SAINT LOUIS, MISSOURI 63118-3968

Editorial assistants: Mary D. Jackson and Phoebe W. Wellman

Write to Library for the Blind, 1333 S. Kirkwood Road, St. Louis, MO 63122-7295 to obtain *The Last Word* (Teachers Guide) in braille or sightsaving print for the visually impaired.

Unless otherwise stated, the Scripture quotations in this publication are from the Holy Bible: NEW INTERNATIONAL VERSION, copyright ©1973, 1978, 1984 by the International Bible Society. Used by permission of Zondervan Bible Publishers.

Bible quotations marked RSV are from the Revised Standard Version of the Bible, copyrighted 1946, 1952, © 1971, 1972, 1973 by the Division of Christian Education of the National Council of Churches of Christ in the U.S.A., and are used by permission.

Bible quotations marked TEV are from the Good News Bible, the Bible in *Today's English Version.* Copyright © American Bible Society 1966, 1971, 1976, used by permission.

Scripture quotations marked NASB are from the NEW AMERICAN STANDARD BIBLE, © The Lockman Foundation 1960, 1962, 1963, 1968, 1971, 1972, 1973, 1975, and are used by permission.

The quotations from the Lutheran Confessions in this publication are from *The Book of Concord: The Confessions of the Ev. Lutheran Church,* ed. by Theodore G. Tappert, Fortress Press ©1959. Used by permission of the publisher.

Copyright © 1989 Concordia Publishing House 3558 S. Jefferson Avenue, St. Louis, MO 63118-3968.

ISBN: 978-0-7586-5046-7

All rights reserved. No part of this publication may be reproduced, stored in a retrieval system, or transmitted, in any form or by any means, electronic, mechanical, photocopying, recording, or otherwise, without the prior written permission of Concordia Publishing House.

Contents

To the Teacher 4
Chapter 1: The Letter to the Hebrews 6
    1. The Last Word 6
    2. Hang Tough 7
    3. Superior to Angels 8
    4. Superior to Moses 10
    5. Superior to the Old Testament Priests 11
    6. A Better Way 13
    7. A Better Sanctuary 14
    8. A Better Sacrifice 16
    9. Searching Scripture 17
    10. Our Response to Jesus' Better Way 18
    11. Heroes of the Faith 19
    12. The Race to Mount Zion 21
    13. Faith Responds to God's Love 22
    14. The Letter to the Hebrews: A Review 24
    15. Test: The Letter to the Hebrews 27
Chapter 2: The Letter of James 31
    16. Living the Faith 31
    17. Brother of the Lord 32
    18. The Royal Law: Love 33
Chapter 3: 1 Peter 34
    19. Born Again for Hopeful Living 34
    20. Chosen to be Used and to Live as Strangers 36
    21. Chosen to be Baptized 38
Chapter 4: 2 Peter and Jude 40
    22. Twin Letters 40
    23. The Know-Nothings 41
Chapter 5: The Three General Epistles of John 43
    24. The Love Letters of John 43
    25. Children of the Heavenly Father 44
    26. Smile! God Loves You! 46
    27. The Second and Third Letters 47
    28. The General Epistles: A Review 49
    29. Test: The General Epistles 51
Chapter 6: The Revelation of St. John 55
    30. The Mystery Book of the New Testament 55
    31. Clues for Solving the Mystery 56
    32. Preparing for the Truth 58
    33. Setting the Stage 61
    34. Tribulations That Are to Come—First Cycle 63
    35. Tribulations That Are to Come—Second Cycle 64
    36. What's a Nice Person Like You Doing in This Kind of World? 66
    37. The Gathering Storm 67
    38. The War Intensifies 69
    39. Tribulations That Are to Come—Third Cycle 70
    40. The Fall of Babylon 72
    41. The Victory Celebration 73
    42. The Millennium 74
    43. The New Jerusalem 76
    44–45. The Revelation of St. John: Review and Test 77

To the Teacher

The Last Word has been designed for 12th-grade students, but it may be taught (with adaptations) in grades 9, 10, or 11.

To provide flexibility and to accommodate various teaching and learning styles, *The Last Word* is organized into chapters that are divided into sections. Ordinarily a teacher will teach one section per class session. At times, however, student interest and discussion of a topic may lead a teacher to spend two or more class sessions on a given section. At other times a teacher may choose to cover more than one section in a given class period.

For variety a teacher may choose to assign certain sessions to individuals or small groups for reports in class. Or, if time does not allow for all the material to be covered in the course of a semester, sections may be selected for the time available.

THE LUTHERAN HIGH SCHOOL RELIGION SERIES

This is one of 12 courses for Lutheran high schools. The courses have been designed for a variety of scheduling programs. Four courses contain 90 sessions each and provide materials for 5 sessions per week for one semester. Each of the other 8 courses contains 45 sessions and is designed for one quarter (half a semester).

The following is a list of the 12 courses:

Grade 9
- [ ] *Fitting In: Relationships with God and Others* (45 sessions)
- [ ] *For God So Loved . . . : A Study of the Gospel of John* (45 sessions)
- [ ] *God's Old Testament People* (90 sessions)

Grade 10
- [ ] *God's Plan Unfolds: The Church from Nazareth to Nicaea* (90 sessions)
- [ ] *One Body in Christ: A Study of the Church* (45 sessions)
- [ ] *Instruments in God's Hands: A Study of Christian Ethics* (45 sessions)

Grade 11
- [ ] *Saved by Grace: A Study of Christian Doctrine* (90 sessions)
- [ ] *The Church Takes Shape: A Study of Church History* (45 sessions)
- [ ] *Which Way Is the Right Way? A Study of Christianity, Cults, and Other Religions* (45 sessions)

Grade 12
- [ ] *Choices, Choices, Choices: Managing My Life* (90 sessions)
- [ ] *Commitment: God's Plan for Engagement and Marriage* (45 sessions)
- [ ] *The Last Word: Hebrews, the General Epistles, and the Revelation of St. John* (45 sessions)

This curriculum was prepared after a survey of all high schools affiliated with the Association for Lutheran Secondary Schools and after extensive conversations with high school and college teachers. Thus it reflects both current practices and theory. The Parish Services staff wishes to express a special word of thanks to the ALSS administrators for their cooperation and assistance.

While any course assumes a certain background and maturity of the students, each course can stand alone—a previous course in this series is not an *absolute* prerequisite. The Student Books contain no grade-level designations; therefore courses can be adapted to other grade levels.

MATERIALS

In addition to this guide, you will need a copy of the accompanying Student Book and a Bible. (This course generally quotes the New International Version of the Bible. We recommend that you select a translation commonly used in the congregations of your students.)

The students will need a copy of the Student Book and a Bible. They will also need access to other resources, such as Bible dictionaries and concordances.

USING THIS GUIDE

Some sessions suggest more activities than can be accomplished in one period. Be selective. You know your students. Use the activities and materials that will be of most value to them.

HOMEWORK

Many pages of this course will contain questions. These questions ask for information that most students can complete outside of class. If you make regular homework assignments, you might ask students to complete these questions in advance.

LAW AND GOSPEL

The plans in this guide help you structure sessions so that students see both Law and Gospel. Pray for the Holy Spirit to work in them as they hear God's words of accusation, forgiveness, and guidance. As you begin to plan the course, you might reread *The Proper Distinction Between Law and Gospel* by C. F. W. Walther. This is good reading for all who work with youth, especially teachers.

Once **(John 12:20–21)** some Greeks came to

Philip and said, **"Sir, we would like to see Jesus."** Your basic goal as you teach each day should be to bring students to see Jesus. Confront them with their spiritual needs; then lead them to see Jesus their Savior as the answer to those needs. Let His love permeate all relationships in your classroom as you grow together in grace by the Spirit's power. Set this as your primary goal, and let all other objectives proceed from this goal.

We invite you to write the editors about *The Last Word: Hebrews, the General Epistles, and the Revelation of St. John*. Share the joys and frustrations you experienced as you taught this course, offer suggestions for other courses, etc. Please send your comments to

Editorial Services Unit
Board for Parish Services
The Lutheran Church—Missouri Synod
1333 South Kirkwood Road
St. Louis, MO 63122-7295

CHAPTER 1
THE LETTER TO THE HEBREWS

1. The Last Word

CENTRAL TRUTH

Though frequently neglected in the church, the last nine books of the New Testament have certain unique characteristics that make them especially meaningful for in-depth study by maturing young people.

OBJECTIVES

That the students by the power of the Spirit will

1. recognize the unique importance of last words;
2. identify those New Testament books that were the last to be written;
3. affirm the importance of *every* word of Scripture;
4. compare and contrast the situation of the Church between its birth and its maturation;
5. note the challenges facing a maturing Christian church or individual;
6. explain the difference between antilegomena and homologoumena;
7. recognize that the antilegomena went through a unique testing period in the church;
8. note the difference between general writings and those of a more specific nature;
9. be motivated to hear God speak to them in these, the last of His written words.

BACKGROUND

The course is based on the presupposition that the Holy Scriptures in their entirety and in every particular are the Word of God. As the Lutheran Confessions affirm, "We pledge ourselves to the prophetic and apostolic writings of the Old and New Testaments as the pure and clear fountain of Israel, which is the only true norm according to which all teachers and teachings are to be judged and evaluated" (FC SD Rule and Norm 3).

While it is certainly true that the Almighty God can speak to His people today in other ways, all spiritual insights must be judged according to the clear words of Scripture. Jesus makes it clear that Scripture is our ultimate authority and is sufficient for all that we need to know for our salvation.

In a parable, Jesus spoke of the rich man in hell who in his misery asked Father Abraham to give his brothers on earth a special revelation so that they might escape eternal condemnation. Father Abraham responded, "**They have Moses and the Prophets; let them listen to them**" (Luke 16:29). In his letter to Timothy, St. Paul described the completeness and sufficiency of Scripture thus, "**And how from infancy you have known the holy Scriptures, which are able to make you wise for salvation through faith in Christ Jesus. All Scripture is God-breathed [inspired] and is useful for teaching, rebuking, correcting and training in righteousness, so that the man of God may be thoroughly equipped for every good work**" (2 Tim. 3:15–17).

Today we all are exposed to the claims of many self-appointed spokespersons for God who profess that they have received all manner of private words from God. We need to explore the concept of the Bible being God's last Word to us in the context of the final authority, sufficiency, completeness, and clarity of Scripture as God's Word to us.

INTRODUCTION (Objective 1)

As you read through the introductory paragraph with the class, encourage students to give additional examples that illustrate the special significance of last words.

Answers to the six quotations provided are (1) Patrick Henry; (2) Porky Pig; (3) Douglas MacArthur; (4) Jesus; (5) Julius Caesar; (6) Martin Luther. A brief game might be made of other suggestions from the class.

GOD'S LAST WORDS (Objectives 2 and 3)

Refer to the time line in the Student Book and identify those books which are to be studied in this course. Point out that, with the exception of **James**, all of these books came into being at least 30 years after the birth of the Christian church on Pentecost.

It will be important to emphasize that no claim is being made for the superiority of these books over others in the Bible. Rather, the unique history of these writings should be taken into account and their special features appreciated.

WORDS FOR A MATURING CHURCH (Objectives 4 and 5)

As you work through this section with the class, help students to see that Christians gradually incurred the opposition of society and were cruelly persecuted, especially late in the first century. Early persecutions were localized and largely limited to opposition from unbelieving Jews. With the persecution by Nero, Christians had even become victims of the government of the Roman Empire itself.

Note also that false teachings began to creep into the church. These caused additional stresses (see **3 John; Jude**).

The impending loss of the physical presence of the apostles to guide them was an additional burden. Now Christians had to be independent of the apostles' physical leadership (although their guidance would continue to be available through the books of the New Testament). This loss is certainly worth exploring with young people; many of whom are struggling with the challenges of a growing independence from the security of parental control.

SPOKEN AGAINST (Objectives 6 and 7)

The development of the New Testament canon is covered well in an earlier course in this series, *God's Plan Unfolds: The Church from Nazareth to Nicea.* Although students ought to be somewhat familiar with this history, some review will be necessary. The teacher should be acquainted with the material presented in the previous course. An important resource for the teacher of this course is Martin H. Franzmann's, *The Word of the Lord Grows* (St. Louis: Concordia, 1961). This book is a good investment for the teacher's personal library.

Don't get bogged down in the material in this section. It is enough for students to understand that these books were only gradually accepted after the most careful, critical scrutiny. This fact can strengthen one's confidence in these particular books.

GOD'S GIFTS FOR EVERYONE (Objective 8)

With the students, page through the epistles of Paul, noting the addressees for each of the letters. Help students note that these letters are addressed either to individuals or to specific congregations. A quick survey of the opening verses of the books to be studied in this course will show that, with a few exceptions, they were intended originally for a much wider audience.

"DON'T JUST DO SOMETHING—SIT THERE" (Objective 9)

This section speaks for itself. Make much of the play on words!

2. Hang Tough

CENTRAL TRUTH

The letter to the Hebrews, which holds many historical mysteries, contains a unified message that clearly calls Christians to hold firmly to the precious Gospel of grace because it is infinitely superior to all Law-oriented, man-made plans of salvation.

OBJECTIVES

That the students by the power of the Spirit will

1. recognize the importance of the spiritual decisions they are making at this time in their lives;
2. reaffirm their commitment to the Gospel of Christ;
3. state some of the problems involved in identifying the writer of the letter to the Hebrews;
4. demonstrate a knowledge of the approximate date of the letter along with the reasons for that belief;
5. explain why it is believed that the letter was written to Hebrew Christians at Rome;
6. recognize the general outline of the letter to the Hebrews;
7. summarize the problems facing the Hebrew Christians of Rome;
8. acknowledge their need of encouragement in the Christian faith at this time in their lives.

BACKGROUND

A clear understanding of the proper distinction between Law and Gospel is an absolute necessity for a teacher who proposes to guide young people through the Word of God. A small book which would be very helpful is Walter C. Pieper's *God's No and God's Yes* (St. Louis: Concordia, 1961).

Some commentaries place Hebrews into the category of general, or catholic, epistles which are addressed to a wide audience. **Hebrews** does not belong to that group because it obviously was written to a well-defined group of people in a specific place (see **13:23–24**). The general epistles are addressed to a wider audience.

As a teacher, resist the temptation to become overly involved in the technicalities of the dating, authorship, and destination of the book. This material needs to be discussed, but it is quite speculative, and therefore dare not become the central thought of the lesson.

The Septuagint translation mentioned in the text, the pre-Christian Greek version of the Old Testament, is so called because of the legend that the translation was made about 270 B.C. for Ptolemy II of Egypt by 72 scholars from Jerusalem.

INTRODUCTION (Objectives 1 and 2)

You might want to begin by calling attention to the session title, "Hang Tough." Ask students under what circumstances they might use that expression and what it means to them. Lead from there to an examination of the opening paragraphs.

Discuss briefly with students the implications of Jesus' warning about the danger of looking back. Be careful not to allow this admonition to degenerate into a moralistic discourse on how Christians should behave. It is merely to demonstrate the need for forward progress in the faith.

The parable of the sower and the seed likewise

could easily consume the entire period. Rather, focus on the seed that began to grow rapidly, but in difficult times did not have the root system to sustain it. Again, the emphasis is faith in God, trusting in the effective power of His Word.

Encourage the class to share some of the major decision-making that is going on in their lives right now. Do not be shocked if some of them express serious doubts about their faith or their church membership. These young people are "testing the waters" of many parts of their lives—including the spiritual.

THE WRITER OF THE LETTER (Objective 3)

Have students page through the other letters of the New Testament, and note specific mention of the writers. Work through the questions with the class. Expected answers are the following:

1. He is obviously Jewish because he includes the Old Testament Hebrews as his forefathers.

2. He makes it clear that he did not receive his information about the Gospel from Christ, but from "those who heard Him." This excludes any of the apostles (and also Paul) from consideration.

3. The book is filled with such references. It certainly indicates that the writer had much more than a passing acquaintance with the Old Testament and with Jewish ceremonial customs.

4. He is apparently well-known to Timothy and, as such, must have associated with companions of St. Paul.

Apollos is probably still the best guess as to the human writer. The description of him and his training would fit the requirements. In addition, he was from Alexandria, a center of Greek learning and thought. Do not push the issue; the main point is that the Holy Spirit is the ultimate Author. The Bible has many writers, but only one Author. The Student Book is careful to use the two terms distinctly.

THE DATE OF THE LETTER (Objective 4)

Work through this section with the class, being sure to have students look up the Scripture references. Point out the position of **Hebrews** on the time line at the beginning of session 1.

THE DESTINATION OF THE LETTER (Objective 5)

The letter can be most easily understood if the destination is Rome. Of course, scholars debate this, but the evidence for a Roman destination is the strongest. Nero's persecution did not descend suddenly on the church in Rome like the judgment day, but it did grow in intensity during the years immediately following 64. This would account for the persecution which had not yet resulted in bloodletting.

AN OUTLINE OF THE LETTER (Objective 6)

Do not take too much time with this section. It is intended to give students a general picture of the book they will study in detail later. Page through the letter with students, pointing out the beginning and ending of each section.

THE PURPOSE OF THE LETTER (Objectives 7 and 8)

This section is intended to be the heart of the lesson. Be sure to allow enough time to read and discuss it as thoroughly as possible. Perhaps the ten passages could be assigned to small groups seated near each other. Each group could then report their findings to the class. If time runs short, the passages might be assigned for the following day.

ASSIGNMENT

Ask students to read the entire letter to the Hebrews. Explain that this is meant to be a rapid overview and not an in-depth study. A feeling for the entire book is very valuable in any Bible study and the time spent for this overview will be worthwhile. The reading should take about an hour; therefore, you may want to make this a two-day assignment. Encourage students to approach this as an opportunity to let God speak to them rather than as just another class assignment.

3. Superior to Angels

CENTRAL TRUTH

Jesus, as the very Word of God, is the ultimate revelation of God to humankind. To rely on any other source for one's understanding of God is unnecessary and spiritually disastrous.

OBJECTIVES

That the students by the power of the Spirit will

1. demonstrate a knowledge of the functions of the prophetic office in Scripture;
2. recognize the significance of Jesus as the "Word made flesh";
3. summarize the ways in which Christ is superior to all other messengers from God;
4. explain the way that angels function as messengers in Scripture and be able to give specific examples;
5. recognize the many worldly messengers which influence the religious convictions of people today;
6. affirm their loyalty to Christ and the Gospel as the best revelation of God.

BACKGROUND

In the prologue to John's gospel, Jesus is identified as being "the Word." The Greek word used is *logos* and has come to be used when speaking of the second person of the Trinity. This terminology is significant in this lesson which shows the Lord as God's message as well as messenger to the human family. A person's words originate in the person and, in the same way, Christ comes from God. He reveals the thoughts and feelings of God in the same way that the words of human persons reveal their inner ideas and emotions.

Not only the words spoken by Jesus, but His entire personality, His way of dealing with people, His smile or His frown, and everything about Him was a way chosen by God to communicate with people.

The message of Jesus is that which we have in the Bible. Although God certainly could reveal Himself to us in any way He might choose, He chose to give us the Holy Scriptures as the only reliable source of His revelation to us. Our Lutheran Confessions make this clear in the Formula of Concord.

It is apparent to any student of the Bible that certain numbers have a distinctive significance, as will become more clear in our study of **Revelation** later. The number seven seems to be of special importance; it might be good to point out to students the seven characteristics of Jesus listed in **Heb. 1:2b–3**. There are also seven Old Testament quotations given as evidence in **1:5a–13**. While there are many theories about this number, it seems to be used to indicate God's covenant with people.

Hebrews 1 and **2** serve as an introduction to sessions 3–5. Jesus is shown to be superior to angels, Moses, and the Old Testament priests. It might be helpful to relate this discussion to the threefold office of Christ as prophet, priest, and king in the following way:

1. Christ as prophet—brings God's message to people.
   Angels—bring God's messages.
2. Christ as priest—intercedes for people. God offered Himself as the sacrifice for sin, and keeps the Law for us.
   Old Testament Priests—interceded for the people, offered animal sacrifices, and kept ceremonial laws.
3. Christ as King—rules over all things.
   Moses—is remembered as the Law-giver and leader.

This threefold office may also be related to the seven characteristics of God's Son in **1:2b–3** in the following ways:
1. Heir implies kingship.
2. Creation shows power and kingly authority.
3. Radiance or illumination is prophetic work.
4. Representation can be prophetic or priestly work.
5. Sustaining others is certainly the function of a king.
6. Providing purification is a priestly function.
7. The right hand of the Father is kingly power and priestly intercession.

SUPERIOR TO ANGELS

Read through this section with students and look up the Bible references. You might challenge students to find other examples of angels as messengers. Avoid references to "the angel of the Lord," as this expression probably refers to Christ Himself before His incarnation (see also **Gen. 22:11–12**).

IN FULFILLMENT OF THE PROMISES

While reading **Heb. 1:4–14** with students, have them identify the Old Testament passages being quoted. Margin references in their Bibles will be necessary and you may have to assist some. Answers are (1) **Ps. 2:7**, (2) **2 Sam. 7:14**, (3) **Ps. 97:7**, (4) **Ps. 104:4**, (5) **Ps. 45:6–7**, (6) **Ps. 102:25–27**, (7) **Ps. 110:1**.

A WORD OF CAUTION

Work through this section with the class. The questions could be assigned as homework, but class discussion is suggested. Here is a list of the expected answers:

1. The Law. Angels are often associated with the giving of the Law.

2. The Gospel. Be sure to point out the superiority of the Gospel.

3. (a) Eyewitness of the apostles; (b) Signs, wonders, miracles; (c) Gifts of the Holy Spirit.

4. **Ps. 8:4–6**.

5. He humbled Himself and became a man. In this, His state of humiliation, He did not always and fully use His divine power.

6. He did this so that He might take our place under the Law and suffer and die for our sin.

7. Various responses will be meaningful.

THE MESSENGERS OF TODAY

Discussion of this section is an opportunity to invite students to give examples of people today who base their religious beliefs on something other than the Word. For example, some TV evangelists claim to receive private messages from God in their prayer towers. Entire groups such as the Mormons base their beliefs on revelations given by God to their "prophets." The papacy claims direct revelation. Science serves as the basis for many people's convictions about the existence of God and the creation of the world. Many young people believe because "that's what my dad or mom told me."

It is very important for young people to recognize the source of their own beliefs and the beliefs of others, and to subject all beliefs to the authority of the Word of God. The daily newspaper will provide many examples to make this discussion relevant.

4. Superior to Moses

CENTRAL TRUTH
Jesus, the Kings of kings, is the only leader for Christians to follow as they travel through the wilderness of this life to the promised land of rest in the Gospel.

OBJECTIVES
By the grace of God students will

1. acknowledge Jesus as King and commit to following Him;
2. recognize that faithful following implies willing obedience;
3. demonstrate their faith by godly living;
4. express joy in the Gospel which gives rest from the burdensome demands of the Law;
5. look forward to eventual eternal rest in heaven with Jesus.

BACKGROUND
In the last lesson we stressed the prophetic office of Christ as the Word of God as He was compared to the angelic messengers. Today as we call attention to His function as King, we will compare His leadership with that of Moses. As King, Jesus has **"all authority in heaven and on earth" (Matt. 28:18).** This authority is usually described in terms of the following three kingdoms:

    a. Kingdom of power: the entire universe including all creatures, visible and invisible.

    b. Kingdom of grace: all true believers on earth who have accepted God's grace through faith.

    c. Kingdom of glory: all who are in heaven.

These three realms are closely related in that they have the same King and serve the same purpose—the salvation of God's people. Christ rules the universe for the benefit of believers. In **Rom. 8:28** we read, **"We know that in all things God works for the good of those who love Him, who have been called according to His purpose."** In fact, the only reason God has for allowing the world to continue is to allow opportunity for more people to become a part of the Kingdom of grace **(2 Peter 3:9).** And the only function of the Kingdom of grace is to recruit and prepare people for the Kingdom of glory (**Matt. 28:18–20**).

In order to understand the impact of a comparison between Jesus and Moses on first century Hebrews, one must be aware of the stature of Moses in Jewish theology. The exodus of Israel from Egypt is undoubtedly the central event of the Old Testament. It is the symbol by which all of the following events were interpreted. To the Hebrews Moses and the Exodus were inseparable.

God Himself spoke of the uniqueness of Moses when He castigated Aaron and Miriam in **Num. 12:6–8, "When a prophet of the Lord is among you, I reveal Myself to him in visions, I speak to him in dreams. But this is not true of My servant Moses; he is faithful in all My house. With him I speak face to face, clearly and not in riddles; he sees the form of the Lord. Why then were you not afraid to speak against My servant Moses?"**

The Messiah, it was promised, would be a prophet like Moses **(Deut. 18:15).** In the parallelism of Hebrew poetry Moses was even used to represent the entire nation of Israel **(Ps. 103:7).** Jewish people living in the New Testament period believed that God had revealed His will and His laws through Moses, and therefore that Moses was the ultimate authority for all religious matters. Many also seemed to have believed that through ordination the spirit of Moses was transmitted to the scribes as his successors.

A clear understanding of the cause/effect relationship between justification and sanctification is absolutely essential if this lesson is to have a Gospel orientation. In the discussion of faith and works, students must understand that obedience comes as a result of faith through the working of the Holy Spirit in the regenerated believer. Faith and works go together like a horse and carriage—you can't have one without the other.

Faith must precede works, because **"without faith it is impossible to please God" (Heb. 11:6).** Works must follow faith, because **"As the body without the spirit is dead, so faith without deeds is dead" (James 2:26).** The emphasis must be on spirit-motivated, joyful, willing obedience to Jesus in gratitude for His undeserved love toward us sinners.

FOLLOW THE LEADER (Objectives 1 and 2)
Begin by checking student progress on the assignment given in session 2—the reading of the entire book of **Hebrews.** This should be completed by now. Discuss any comments or questions the class may have, but avoid detailed examination of texts which will be studied later.

Use this section to review the central thought of the previous lesson and as an introduction to today's comparison of Jesus and Moses.

Also use this section for the basis of a discussion about the place of Moses in Jewish thinking. It is important to have students look up Bible references and apply them. Share as much of the background material on Jesus' kingly office as time allows.

BELIEVING IS BEHAVING
(Objectives 2 and 3)

Have students identify the psalm quoted in the text **(Ps. 95:7–11).** Discuss this section thoroughly. Encourage students to provide examples of Israel's disobedience and lack of faith. The discussion of this warning can become very legalistic unless time is taken to work through the cause/effect relationship of justification and sanctification. Solicit student suggestions as to ways in which we can "encourage one another daily" in Christian living. How does a young Christian do this without being classified as a religious freak?

Make much of the close relationship between unbelief and disobedience in **verses 12, 18,** and **19.** Turn the discussion in a positive direction by relating faith to obedience.

A SABBATH REST (Objectives 4 and 5)

It is important that this lesson be planned so that there is adequate time to spend on this last section. Here is the chance to emphasize God's grace and finish the session on a joyful, optimistic Gospel note.

Joshua leading the people into the promised land is a beautiful symbol of Jesus leading Christians into His rest. Many students will be surprised to learn that these two names are identical. Ask for examples of other names which have a different pronunciation in another language, i.e. John-Hans-Juan, Mary-Maria, Robert-Roberto, James-Jaime, etc.

Be sure that students understand that God's promise is not only for the future, but is for each of us now—TODAY. Christians have much more than "pie in the sky when they die."

You may introduce the subject of sabbath rest by pointing out that from the time of Adam and Eve people observed times for rest and worship. But at Mount Sinai God established the seventh day as the day of rest and worship for Israel. It was to remind Israel of God as their Creator and Lord *(Ex. 20:8–11)* and to serve as a time for them to recall their deliverance from Egypt by the Lord. It was a time to mediate on God's Word—a time to praise and worship Him for His gift of salvation.

The day was a time to remember God's deliverance, a time to praise and worship Him for His gift of salvation. Faith in the Gospel does the same for the Christian today. It frees one from the burden of the Law. It motivates active pursuit of godly living. Smile as you teach this!

GLORY LAND

Students may enjoy closing this session with the joyful, upbeat song, "Glory Land." Guitar accompaniment will add much to the singing.

ASSIGNMENT

Ask students to choose either **Matt. 13:3–23** or **John 15:1–8** and answer the following question: "How does this Bible reference apply to me as I rest in the Gospel?"

5. Superior to the Old Testament Priests

CENTRAL TRUTH

Jesus, the High Priest of God's people, is the only Mediator to represent us before the throne of God. Under the Gospel, any other priestly intercession is unnecessary and useless.

OBJECTIVES

That the students by the power of the Spirit will

1. summarize the functions of the Old Testament priesthood;
2. understand that Jesus perfectly accomplishes every goal of the priesthood;
3. recognize Jesus as superior to any other intercessor—past, present, or future;
4. desire to progress from the elementary truths of Scripture to mature, in-depth contact with more complicated theological issues;
5. recount how Melchizedek in Scripture serves as a symbol of Christ;
6. rejoice in the knowledge of Jesus as their representative in heaven;
7. resolve to make full and confident use of Jesus' intercession as they face the challenges of life.

BACKGROUND

The Priesthood

The office of priest did not exist in the early days of man's relationship with God. Each person established his own communication with Him. Cain and Abel, as well as the patriarchs who followed them, offered their own sacrifices and prayers. When the Hebrew nation was organized at Sinai, however, God ordered the establishment of the office of priest. Aaron and his sons were appointed to that office and only his descendants were eligible to hold the position. In fact, *all* of his male descendants were priests unless disqualified because of some defect **(Lev. 21:16–23).**

At first the duties of the priest included offering prayers and sacrifices to God on behalf of the people **(Lev. 16:5–25),** teaching the Law **(Lev. 10:11),** discerning God's will in national decisions through the use of the sacred lots—Urim and Thummin **(Ex. 28:30),** seeing to it that all ceremonial laws were carried out **(Lev. 18:1–5),** and blessing the people **(Num. 6:22–27).** However, with the later emergence of the office of prophet, the role of God's spokesperson and teacher was no longer seen as a priestly function.

By the time of Christ the priest functioned basically as the only access that people had to God. It might be that Jesus' disciples asked Him to teach them how to pray **(Luke 11:1)** because they had been isolated from God by this intervening priesthood.

The Unforgivable Sin

In **Heb. 6:4–8** you will encounter the very difficult teaching sometimes called "the sin against the Holy Spirit." It will come up again in **chapter 10:26–31** and so it is important to be as informed as possible.

In His response to the Pharisees who had accused Him of doing miracles by the power of Satan, Jesus said, **"And so I tell you, every sin and blasphemy will be forgiven men, but the blasphemy against the Spirit will not be forgiven" (Matt. 12:31).** This is a sin directed against the very work of the Holy Spirit who through the Gospel is working faith in the heart. When a person, even though he is convinced of its truthfulness, rejects the Gospel from pure spite and malice, he is making the Holy Spirit's work of conversion impossible. When every attempt made by the Spirit to draw one to Christ is resisted for no other reason than stubborn refusal, it is simply impossible to win that person.

It sometimes happens that Christians worry for fear that they have committed this sin, but such concern is unfounded. Anyone who is committing this sin would not in the least be concerned about it. Only the Holy Spirit could create such concern in the heart; therefore, a person who is concerned about faith has not shut Him out.

This sin is not unforgivable because it is too great. No sin is beyond the forgiving grace of God. The problem is that it makes repentance impossible and willful impenitence is never forgiven.

The unforgivable nature of this sin continues only as long as the heart condition that defines it. Be sure to note that the New International Version footnote to **Heb. 6:6** indicates another acceptable translation of this difficult passage. The passage, beginning at **verse 4,** would then read, **"It is impossible for those who have once been enlightened . . . if they fall away, to be brought back to repentance, WHILE to their loss they are crucifying . . ."** This makes it more clear that repentance is impossible only as long as the person continues in this sin.

Melchizedek

This mysterious person is mentioned only three times in the Bible but plays an important part in the argument in **Hebrews** for the superiority of Christ. His name means "king (Melchi) of righteousness (zedek)," and he is introduced in **Gen. 14:18** as the king of Salem (which is probably Jerusalem, Uru-salim, "city of peace"). It should also be noted that "Salem" is used as the name of Jerusalem in **Ps. 76:2.** Jerusalem is also on the route from Hobah and Damascus to Hebron, where Abraham was going when he met Melchizedek in **Genesis 14.**

Nothing is recorded about the genealogy of this man, and so he is described as without father or mother. No mention is made of his birth or life. He suddenly emerges from the unknown and just as suddenly disappears.

This Melchizedek was "priest of God Most High." Somehow this king of Salem had come to know and to serve the true God and Abraham acknowledges that by paying him the tithe. This king came from his royal city to welcome Abraham as he returned after rescuing Lot by defeating Kedorlaomer and his allies.

Melchizedek is mentioned again in **Ps. 110:4,** which is a clear reference to the Messiah as a **"a priest forever, in the order of Melchizedek."** This is a passage quoted in the book of **Hebrews.**

In **Hebrews** it is shown what a great person Melchizedek must have been—Abraham, and through him Levi (the priesthood), paid tithes to him, thus admitting their inferiority. So Jesus' identification with Melchizedek (a type or symbol of Christ), demonstrates His superiority over the Old Testament priesthood.

An interesting note on the names and title of Melchizedek and Jesus is this: "Melchizedek" means "King of righteousness" and Jesus is called **"The Lord Our Righteousness" (Jer. 23:6);** also, Melchizedek is the king of Salem (peace) and Jesus is **"Prince of peace" (Is. 9:6).**

INTRODUCTION (Objectives 1 and 2)

Ask students for examples of times when they have felt the need of an intercessor or go-between. Perhaps a young man wants to ask a certain young lady to the prom and so he gets a mutual friend to "prepare the way" by finding out if she is interested in being asked. Sometimes one is reluctant to ask Dad for permission to do something, and so Mom is asked to intercede. Try to involve the students, and then move to the topic of Jesus as our Priest and Intercessor with the Father.

Review the general functions of the Old Testament priesthood as sacrificer and intercessor and briefly draw from the students how Jesus functions in that office for us.

THE GREAT HIGH PRIEST
(Objectives 1, 2, and 3)

When speaking about the curtain in the temple be sure to remind students of the tearing of that curtain on Good Friday.

What are some of the problems of teenagers that Jesus also experienced? Ask students to recall times when Jesus prayed for Himself and for others. When did He shed tears? When did He cry with a loud voice? Marginal references in the Bible will be helpful.

CAUTION: MILK OR MEAT? (Objective 4)

Here is an opportunity to deal with a subject that comes up often among high school students—the need for continuing Bible study throughout life.

Try not to get bogged down in a discussion of the unforgivable sin at this time. The topic will come up again in session 10. Be content if students have a general definition of this danger.

MELCHIZEDEK AND LEVI (Objectives 3 and 5)

Work through this section rather quickly. The student text material serves as a useful outline.

JESUS IS THE BEST (Objectives 6 and 7)

Emphasize Jesus' current function at the right hand of the Father representing us and pleading for us before God. This is not emphasized in the text, but is important for all Christians to remember.

AN ASSIGNMENT

Session 11 will be devoted to a study of the great faith chapter. In some objective way (drawing random numbers, etc.) assign one student to each of the reports listed below. The number following each topic indicates the verse in **Hebrews 11** in which the example is given.

1. Abel **(4)**
2. Enoch **(5–6)**
3. Noah **(7)**
4. Abraham **(8–10)**
5. Abraham **(11–12)**
6. Abraham **(17–19)**
7. Isaac **(20)**
8. Jacob **(21)**
9. Joseph **(22)**
10. Moses' parents **(23)**
11. Moses **(24)**
12. Israelites **(29)**
13. Israelites **(30)**
14. Rahab **(31)**
15. Gideon **(32)**
16. Barak **(32)**
17. Samson **(32)**
18. Jephthah **(32)**
19. David **(32)**
20. Samuel **(32)**

6. A Better Way

CENTRAL TRUTH

God's new covenant is based upon Jesus' atoning sacrifice for sin and is mediated by our Lord at the throne of His Father in heaven. It is a far superior replacement for the Old Covenant given through Moses which required mediation by an earthly priesthood.

OBJECTIVES

That the students by the power of the Spirit will

1. summarize the three ways in which the book of **Hebrews** points to Jesus' WAY as the best;
2. give examples of three different types of covenant;
3. define the word *covenant;*
4. state that the Old Covenant could not solve the human sin problem;
5. recognize that human weakness caused the failure of the Old Covenant;
6. explain four gracious promises of the New Covenant;
7. reaffirm a personal commitment to the Gospel.

BACKGROUND

The concept of "covenant" was deeply ingrained in Hebrew thinking. Some understanding of it is essential to a meaningful reading, not only of the epistle to the **Hebrews,** but of the entire Bible.

A covenant was simply an agreement entered into by two or more individuals and sealed by some outward sign. In very ancient times covenants were sealed by swallowing a drop of each other's blood—a ceremony which has interesting implications for Jesus' description of Holy Communion as "the new covenant in My blood." Often covenants were sealed by setting up pillars of stone **(Gen. 31:44–48),** by exchanging handshakes, or by accepting a portion of salt **(Num. 18:19)**—a practice still followed today by nomads of Palestine.

The Bible contains many examples of covenants between people: Abraham and Abimelech **(Gen. 21:27);** Laban and Jacob **(Gen. 31:44);** Jonathan and David **(1 Sam. 18:3).**

More important are the examples of covenants between God and individuals such as between God and Noah **(Gen. 9:13).** The covenant between God and Abraham **(Gen. 13:14–17)** was often repeated to his descendants and sealed by circumcision.

God also made a covenant with the entire nation of Israel. He promised to continue to be their God and to grant national protection of which a sign was to be the Sabbath **(Ex. 31:16).** However, this was a unilateral covenant made entirely by God; the keeping of His commandments was to be but the response of faith to the many gracious acts and words of the Lord **(Deut. 4:13, 23).**

In contrast to the covenant at Sinai, there was to be a new covenant which was to be of a more spiritual character **(Jer. 31:31–34).** This new covenant is to be received in faith **(Gal. 4:21–31)** and is offered for all nations.

The two tablets of stone on which the Ten Commandments were engraved were called the Tables of the Covenant **(Deut. 9:11),** and the ark which held these tablets was called the ark of the covenant **(Num. 10:33).**

INTRODUCTION (Objective 1)

This section serves as an introduction to the next three sessions. Direct students to the outline of **Hebrews** presented in session 2 and ask them to note that we are beginning the third part of the letter.

Use the discussion questions after students have read the first five verses of **chapter 8.** Expected answers include the following:

1. The throne of God in heaven.

2. His own suffering and death on the cross.

3. A priest had to be descended from the tribe of Levi, but Jesus was of the tribe of Judah.

4. The tabernacle. The temple in Jerusalem.

5. Animal sacrifices, grain offerings, etc.

6. They were intended to symbolize the relationship between God and His people. Accept many different responses. This topic will be dealt with in detail in session 7.

A BETTER COVENANT (Objectives 2 and 3)

Read through this section with the class and solicit other examples of the three types of covenants discussed.

SOMETHING WAS WRONG (Objective 4)

Clearly, when anything is replaced there is the implication that something was lacking. Perhaps students can provide examples from their experience in trading. **Gal. 3:20** makes it clear that in this case a mediator is one who puts something into effect.

IDENTIFYING THE PROBLEM (Objectives 4 and 5)

This prophecy from **Jer. 31:31–34** was proclaimed about 600 B.C. Already then God knew that He was planning a new and better covenant. The old covenant was the third type of covenant. Expressions such as "I will make," "I made," and "I turned away" show that God is the initiator of the covenant. "They did not remain faithful" shows that the Israelites rejected the grace God offered in His covenant.

A NEW DEAL (Objective 6)

This is clearly an example of the third type of covenant. It is very much like a will in which gifts are left to survivors with no conditions. In fact, the Greek word used here has the connotation of last will and testament. This section is the heart of this lesson, your opportunity to make the joy of the Gospel come alive in the classroom.

THE OLD IS OBSOLETE (Objective 4)

Take note of the expression "will soon disappear." The old reliance on the Law for salvation has not disappeared yet; it is still with us. Not only around us, but inside of us dwells a "natural man" who is inclined to return to a system of rules and regulations in the spiritual realm. Not only the Hebrews, but each one of us needs the daily admonition to stand fast.

CHOOSE YOUR MOUNTAIN (Objective 7)

Review once again the difference between the Sinai covenant and the Calvary covenant. The hymn "Come to Calv'ry's Holy Mountain" has been printed as a closing litany which can be read or sung responsively.

7. A Better Sanctuary

CENTRAL TRUTH

Jesus, our representative at the right hand of the Father to intercede for us, is in a much better position to help us than were those priests who could only approach God symbolically in an earthly sanctuary.

OBJECTIVES

That the students will

1. describe the design and furnishings of the Old Testament tabernacle;
2. compare and contrast the design of the Old Testament tabernacle with that of the churches of today;
3. describe the use of the tabernacle in Old Testament worship;
4. compare and contrast the use of the tabernacle with the worship practices in present-day churches;
5. recognize the symbolic meaning of the tabernacle;
6. explain how Jesus' place of ministry is superior to earthly worship centers.

BACKGROUND

The Tabernacle

The tabernacle was a moveable tent used by the Israelites during their wandering in the wilderness after leaving slavery in Egypt. God Himself commanded its construction and gave detailed specifications for its design to Moses on Mount Sinai. It was to be a sanctuary where God would dwell with His people **(Ex. 25:8)**.

The importance of this "Tent of Meeting" is clear from the detailed description in **Exodus 25–40**. The materials used in its construction were, for the most part, available in the immediate vicinity. Acacia wood, the hair and skin of animals, gold, silver, brass, and linen furnished by the people through their offerings. The hides of sea cows from the Red Sea were also used.

The tabernacle itself was a rectangle, 45 feet long and 15 feet wide with a curtained entrance at the eastern end. The other three sides were made of boards and the top was covered with a roof of animal skins. The interior was divided into two compartments—the sanctuary (holy place) which was 30 feet in length and the Holy of Holies (Most Holy Place) which was 15 feet square. These two rooms were separated by a very thick curtain.

The tabernacle was positioned in a rectangular courtyard enclosed by a 7½ foot high fence with an entrance at the eastern end. This courtyard measured 150 feet by 75 feet and was open at the top.

The Most Holy Place contained only the ark of

the covenant whose golden lid (the mercy seat) featured the carved figures of cherubim; it represented the very presence of an unapproachable God. The ark contained the stone tablets of the Ten Commandments from Sinai, a sample of the manna with which God fed the people in the wilderness, and the miraculous rod of Aaron which blossomed to confirm the authority of Moses.

The jar of manna and Aaron's rod were missing by Solomon's time **(1 Kings 8:9)**, probably lost when the ark was captured by the Philistines **(1 Sam. 4:10–11)**. The stone tablets and the ark itself were lost later, perhaps when Nebuchadnezzar burned the temple **(2 Kings 25:8–9)**.

The altar of incense stood in the sanctuary directly in front of the curtain that separated it from the Holy of Holies. In this area also stood the table of showbread with its 12 loaves representing the 12 tribes and the golden lampstand with its 7 oil lamps.

The altar of burnt offering for the animal sacrifices and the laver for the ceremonial washing of the priest before entering the tabernacle proper stood outside of the tabernacle but within the courtyard.

This tabernacle remained a central feature of Hebrew worship, even after the Israelites had entered the Promised Land. When Solomon built the permanent temple in Jerusalem, he followed the basic design of the tabernacle except that all of its dimensions were doubled.

What is especially significant in the present study is the differing levels of approach to God represented in the tabernacle. Only Israelites could enter the courtyard, only ordained priests were allowed to enter the tabernacle, and only the High Priest could enter the Most Holy Place—and this only once each year on the Day of Atonement (Yom Kippur). At Mount Sinai a similar distinction was made when the people were restrained from going beyond the foot of the mountain **(Ex. 19:12, 17)**, the priests and 70 elders were permitted to make a closer approach than most of the people **(Ex. 24:9–11)**, but only Moses was permitted to enter into the very presence of the Almighty **(Ex. 24:12–18)**.

Christian Church Design

The earliest Christian houses of worship made use of a common building style in wide use in the Roman Empire—the basilica. This was used for public meetings of all types. Possibly Christians were allowed to use these basilicas for worship before they had their own buildings. When they began to construct their own churches, they followed the same basic plan. Although many changes have taken place in ecclesiastical architecture through the centuries, the floor plan remains largely unchanged. Note the similarities between this basilica design and the Old Testament tabernacle.

The basilica model had three main parts. In front of the entrance is the atrium (narthex). The nave has the form of a rectangle. In the east end of the nave is an elevated chancel area which includes a further elevated platform known as the sanctuary. The chancel was once closed off entirely from the nave by a "rood screen" which is no longer in general use. However, an altar rail remains.

The baptismal font was at first located at the western end of the nave to represent entrance into the faith, but was moved to the vicinity of the chancel at the time of the Reformation to emphasize the relationship between Holy Communion, Baptism, and the Gospel as the means of grace. The altar is the only furnishing on the sanctuary.

INTRODUCTION

Use this section to introduce the central truth of this lesson. Encourage students to share any ideas or experiences they may have with a representative who could not function effectively because of being in the wrong place.

REMEMBERING THE TABERNACLE
(Objectives 1 and 2)

You may reproduce and distribute copies of the tabernacle floor plan included in this Teacher's Guide. If you have an overhead projector available, a transparency will be very effective. Work through the reading from **Heb. 9:1–5** with the class. Refer to the floor plan; fill in as many other details as time permits. The writer says, **"But we cannot discuss these things in detail now" (9:5)**, and that is important for you also to remember. Don't spend an inordinate amount of time on this section!

Ask the students for a description of the differences and similarities between the tabernacle and today's church buildings. Some may be: the altar rail which represents the curtain, the chancel itself which makes one think of the tabernacle, the baptismal font and its connection with the laver, the altar and the ark, etc. Don't go into detail about the meaning of these things now—that will come later. Just discuss structural matters.

THE USE OF THE TABERNACLE
(Objectives 3 and 4)

Make much of the differing levels of approach to God. Share with the class the comparison with the conditions at Sinai as explained in the "Background" section of this Teacher's Guide.

Students will be able to notice many similar practices in their churches: the courtyard (nave) is basically for the people, the chancel is reserved for officiants, the sanctuary is generally approached only by the pastor, etc. Important differences to note include: the chancel is not absolutely restricted to the clergy, the people are not denied visual access to the ceremony, the altar of burnt offering is not represented, etc.

WHAT DOES THIS MEAN? (Objective 5)

Emphasize the opening in the altar rail which is only closed for convenience during the distribution of Holy Communion. The opening represents the tearing of the curtain when Jesus died and is symbolic of the universal priesthood of all believers. Don't fail to make this important point, but be sensitive to the feelings of those students who belong to denominations that still maintain an earthly priesthood and which maintain a solid rail.

THE BEST PLACE (Objective 6)

This section needs little comment. The story of Joseph can be reviewed in **Genesis 42–47**. Remind students of the heroes of faith reports they are working on for session 11.

8. A Better Sacrifice

CENTRAL TRUTH

As our High Priest Jesus has reconciled us to God by voluntarily offering Himself as the only divinely acceptable sacrifice for sin. The promise of the New Covenant has been completely fulfilled and so there is no longer any need to make offerings for sin.

OBJECTIVES

That the students by the power of the Spirit will

1. acknowledge that God's justice demands full payment for sin;
2. recognize the importance of the inner cleansing accomplished by Jesus' sacrificial death;
3. understand the importance of the blood theme in the Gospel;
4. express confidence in the sufficiency of Christ's one-time atonement for all sin;
5. rejoice in the knowledge that Christ's death was completely voluntary;
6. share the Gospel with others.

BACKGROUND

Some understanding of the Old Testament sacrificial system is necessary for an effective teaching of this session. It will be helpful to consult one or more Bible dictionaries. The *Concordia Self-Study Bible* has a very useful chart (p. 150) and many other study Bibles also contain material. Most of the information is found in **Leviticus 1–7** if one chooses to learn first-hand from the original source. What is presented here is a short review of major points.

A significant part of Israelite worship consisted of offerings to God. Public offerings were made on behalf of the entire nation and private offerings were presented by individuals for a number of reasons. There were drink offerings, grain offerings, and animal sacrifices. It is important to note that the shedding of blood was a requirement of every offering, except in the case of the sin offering for the extremely poor; even then it was only acceptable in connection with the blood of the great public altar.

The offerings are usually classified in the following groups:

1. *Burnt offering*—a voluntary offering of a specified animal brought by an individual to present to God as an expression of total dedication to the Lord. The blood of the animal was sprinkled on the altar, and the entire animal was consumed by fire.

2. *Grain offering*—a voluntary offering given in general recognition of God's goodness and favor. It consisted of white meal, unleavened bread, cakes, or roasted ears of corn. It was invariably accompanied by salt. Since no blood was involved, this offering was always made in connection with a burnt offering.

3. *Fellowship offering (peace offering)*—another of the voluntary offerings given to express close communion and fellowship with God. It was done in thanksgiving for some specific blessing, in fulfillment of a vow of some kind, or as a freewill expression of love for God. Any of the acceptable animals was used, but never a bird. After the sprinkling of the blood, part of the meat was given to the priests and the rest was eaten by the person and his friends at the tabernacle.

4. *Sin offering*—a required offering given after one had sinned unintentionally without harming another person. The type of animal sacrificed depended on the status of the person making the offering. The meat was either burnt outside the camp or given to the priests.

5. *Guilt offering*—the required offering given after one had sinned unintentionally, but still harmed another person. A ram or lamb was required. Restitution was also necessary.

There was no offering that could be made in the case of an intentional sin. Intentional sins resulted in either capital punishment or restitution and civil punishments.

Sacrifices involved five sacrificial acts:

1. Presentation of the sacrifice at the door of the sanctuary.

2. Laying on of hands. The person bringing the offering would place his hands on the head of the victim. This was done to indicate that the offering was being dedicated to God, and that the offerer was making it his substitute.

3. Slaying was done by the individual (later by the priests). By this act the person was symbolically accepting the punishment.

4. The application of blood which involved either sprinkling or smearing blood on the altar and pouring it out at its base. In rare cases the blood was smeared on the individual also.

5. The final act of burning. At times the entire

offering was burned; at other times only the fat. But at all times the burning was done so that its essence and flavor would ascend to God.

INTRODUCTION (Objective 1)

This section serves as an introduction to the lesson. Encourage students to supply other examples of unsatisfactory debt payments. It is important to stress the fact that our God is a God of justice as well as a loving and merciful Father. His justice would not permit Him to be satisfied with anything short of full payment for sin.

The Gospel does not offer some kind of cheap grace, but rather it proclaims how God Himself obtained the complete payment for our sin. It was God's justice as well as His love that led Him to offer His own Son as the only sufficient sacrifice for the sins of all people. It was His justice that made the symbolic Old Testament animal sacrifices in themselves inadequate to pay the wages of sin.

NEEDED: AN INNER CLEANSING (Objective 2)

Be certain that students catch the significance of the New Covenant as "the good things that are already here." The good things that Christ has provided under the Gospel are not only blessings for the future, but also for our enjoyment here and now.

The main point of the section is that inner cleansing is a result of Jesus' sacrificial ministry. The **"ashes of a heifer" (v. 13)** were prescribed for the ceremonial cleansing of one who had become unclean through contact with a dead body, human bones, or a grave **(Num. 19)**. Old Testament rituals were never able in themselves to get to the very heart of the problem and provide a thorough cleansing of the conscience. Only the death of Jesus is able to free us completely from the corruption of sin and create a new heart within us. Nothing less than **"the blood of Jesus, His Son, purifies us from all sin" (1 John 1:7)**.

SOMEBODY HAD TO DIE (Objective 3)

Share with the class enough of the material from the background section on the Old Testament sacrifices to show the importance of blood and death in the symbolic ritual of the ancient Israelites.

ONCE IS ENOUGH (Objective 4)

St. Paul, speaking of the death of Christ, says **"The death He died, He died to sin once for all . . ." (Rom. 6:10)**. But by the time of the Reformation, insidious changes had developed in the Christian church.

One significant change was in regard to the people's understanding of the Lord's Supper. Originally this sacrament was instituted by Christ to convey to communicants the assurance of the forgiveness of sins earned by the sacrificial suffering and death of Jesus on the cross. In the Middle Ages, the church began to teach that in the Lord's Supper the priest offered to God a sacrifice in which Christ was crucified anew. Each celebration of the Supper was an offering of the body and blood of Christ to atone for the sins of the people. Thus the once-and-for-all character of Christ's sacrifice on Calvary was debased.

Even today in Roman Catholic churches this sacrificial nature of the Lord's Supper continues to be taught. In spite of the great progress in recent years toward better understanding between Lutherans and Roman Catholics, this point of disagreement continues to be a serious problem.

JESUS TALKS TO HIS FATHER (Objective 5)

In identifying the speaker in **Psalm 40** as Christ Himself, the writer here clearly accepts this psalm as being messianic. Point out to students that since Adam and Eve Jesus is the only person who ever chose to die. Even though human beings may choose the time, place, and manner of their death, no one can escape death itself. Only Jesus had that option.

ICING THE CAKE

This section serves as a summary and closing argument for the entire first part of the epistle, a part often called the doctrinal section. Use this time to review as much as possible what has been said about the superiority of the ministry of Christ and the foolishness of trading Him for something inferior.

WHAT'S THE VERDICT? (Objective 6)

Emphasize the complete sufficiency of the Christian message and the importance of sharing the good news with others.

9. Searching Scripture

REVIEW

This lesson is designed to review some of the major truths which have been presented in the doctrinal section of **Hebrews** and to provide opportunity for students to get into Scripture on their own. The material for this session may be used in one of at least three different ways.

1. It may be assigned as homework after session 8 either collected or discussed in class in session 9.

2. It may be assigned as an activity to be done during the class period for session 9. In that case, students may be asked to work independently, or they might be assigned to small groups. Completed assignments may be collected at the end of the period.

3. It may be used as a group activity with entire

class looking up passages and discussing expected responses.

LAW AND GOSPEL

As indicated in the Student Book, it is not easy to distinguish properly between Law and Gospel. The purpose of this exercise is to help students explain how the content of a given Scripture passage can be either a word of Law or a word of Gospel. How might the passage be heard as promise? How might the message of this same passage be heard as threat or condemnation? You may wish to prepare for this exercise by reviewing Francis Pieper's comments in *Christian Dogmatics,* vol. 1, pp. 76–80; vol. 3, pp. 222–52 (St. Louis: Concordia, 1950, 1953). The classic, of course, is C. F. W. Walther's *The Proper Distinction Between Law and Gospel,* translated by W. H. T. Dau (St. Louis: Concordia, 1929).

PROPHET, PRIEST, OR KING

Is. 9:7	King.
Is. 40:11	King. A shepherd is a ruler and leader.
Is. 53:5–6	Priest. The one who offers a sacrifice.
Micah 5:2	King.
Matt. 5:17	Priest. The keeper of the Law.
Matt. 9:35	Prophet. Bringing God's Word to people.
Matt. 11:27	Prophet. A revealer of God.
Matt. 17:5	Prophet. One to be listened to.
Matt. 28:18	King. He has authority to rule all things.
Mark 1:14	Prophet.
Luke 4:18	Prophet.
Luke 21:5–36	Prophet. Foretelling future events.
John 1:18	Prophet. Making God known to people.
John 10:25	Prophet.
John 12:26	King. Jesus is the leader to follow and serve.
John 17:9	Priest. Our intercessor with the Father.
Rom. 5:19	Priest. Fulfiller of the Law in our place.
Rom. 8:34	Priest.
Eph. 1:21–22	King.
Eph. 5:2	Priest.
Eph. 5:23–24	King.
Phil. 2:10	King.
1 Tim. 2:5	Priest.
1 Peter 3:22	King.
1 John 1:7	Priest. The offerer of the blood sacrifice.
1 John 2:1	Priest.

DIGGING FOR TREASURE

Many students will find this section difficult. Give as much assistance as necessary. Answers will vary widely since no one specific passage is called for.

A REMINDER

Remind students of the assignment on heroes of the faith which they are to prepare for session 11.

10. Our Response to Jesus' Better Way

CENTRAL TRUTH

Jesus is the only solution for our spiritual problems. Therefore we who follow Jesus can meet temptations and persecutions in this world with divine power and confidence as we join hands to share in His victory march.

OBJECTIVES

That the students by the power of the Spirit will

1. acknowledge the necessity of regular worship and fellowship with other Christians;
2. recognize the inconsistency of willful, deliberate sinning after experiencing the grace of God in Christ Jesus;
3. share the joys they have known as young Christians;
4. reaffirm their childhood trust in Jesus;
5. rejoice in the present and future rewards of faith;
6. resolve to avoid any temptation to reject Christ.

INTRODUCTION

This section of **Hebrews** introduces the third and concluding part of the epistle. Refer students to the outline of the letter (session 2) and make certain that they understand the organization of this book.

Read through the Student Book material and encourage class members to give additional comments and examples. Perhaps they themselves have possessions which they seldom use, or they know some person who has foolishly hoarded wealth.

Although there probably will not be enough time to go into great detail about the parables of Jesus mentioned in the Student Book, a brief review (preferably by students) can add much to understanding this lesson.

Be absolutely certain that God's justifying work in Jesus Christ and our response to God's saving activity be kept in the proper perspective. **"We love because He first loved us" (1 John 4:19).** At the same time it must be clear that this response is not optional;

"**faith by itself, if it is not accompanied by action, is dead**" (James 2:17).

A CALL TO PERSEVERE

As you work through this passage with the class, make a list on the chalkboard of the "therefore, since" and the "let us" points. Your list may look something like this:

THEREFORE, SINCE	LET US
we have confidence to enter the Most Holy Place	draw near to God with a sincere heart
by the blood of Jesus	in full assurance of faith
by a new way	hold unswervingly
by a living way	spur one another on
through the curtain	
having a great High Priest	
having hearts cleansed from guilt	
having bodies washed (Baptism)	

MEETING TOGETHER (Objective 1)

This topic is a hot issue today because many people seem to be content to limit their church involvement to watching church services or evangelists on television. Ask students to add examples of what being a Christian without attending church is like. Discuss the joys and privileges of church membership. If students bring up frustrations and disappointments they experience in the congregational life, regard this as a perfect opportunity to explore positive things that each of us can do to **"spur one another on."**

As time permits, investigate the following passages:

Luke 4:16	Ps. 84:10	Ps. 27:4
Luke 24:52–53	Ps. 122:1	Ps. 26:8
Col. 3:16	Gal. 6:6	Col. 2:16–17
Ps. 84:4	1 Cor. 11:24–26	Rom. 14:5–7

PLAYING WITH FIRE (Objective 2)

Do not attempt to sweeten this Law message with a teaspoon of Gospel sugar. Such a mingling of Law and Gospel will only serve to remove the intended bitterness from the Law, and it may even sour the Gospel. This is an opportunity to attack the cavalier attitude toward God's law which infects many Christians today. It is very tempting for young Christians to flirt with the sinful practices of the society in which they live. They should know that they are playing with fire which can be spiritually disastrous.

Verse 29 clearly refers to the **"sin against the Holy Spirit"** which was discussed in an earlier session.

STRENGTH FROM YOUR ROOTS
(Objectives 3 and 4)

As a loving pastor, the writer quickly returns to the positive Gospel motivation which undergirds the Christian life. Encourage students to share their personal experiences in appropriate ways. What temptations have they resisted? What hardships have they endured? Share with students some of your own mountain top experiences as a Christian. As a cyclist gains momentum from going down one hill to help him go up the next, so a Christian gains confidence from past experiences to help him face present challenges to his faith. We go from victory to victory!

CONCENTRATE ON THE REWARD
(Objectives 5 and 6)

Use this section to conclude the session on a high note of confidence. Lead them in a "pep rally" by fixing their eyes on the rewards of following Jesus faithfully.

In the year 1517 amid the spiritual storms stirred by the 95 Theses raging around him, Martin Luther lectured on this part of **Hebrews** to his students. He said, "He who relies on Christ through faith is carried on the shoulders of Christ." How can we shrink back from the temptations and persecutions of the world with such an ally on our side?

A REMINDER

The next session will be devoted to the student reports on the heroes of faith in **Hebrews 11** that have been previously assigned. Be certain that students are getting prepared.

11. Heroes of the Faith

CENTRAL TRUTH

Faith is confident trust in the promises of God without tangible proof. Christians are encouraged in faith by the example of many faithful believers from the past.

OBJECTIVES

That the students by the power of the Spirit will

1. recognize that faith is not just wishful thinking, but solid confidence in God's promises;
2. recognize that faith does not require visible proof;
3. relate the faith example of an Old Testament believer;
4. identify present-day situations which require faith;
5. share examples of faith heroes they have known;
6. express confidence in God's promises to them.

BACKGROUND

The Definition of Faith

The subject of faith in Christ is of supreme importance to Christians. That is not surprising because **"whoever believes in Him is not condemned, but whoever does not believe stands condemned already because he has not believed in the name of God's one and only Son" (John 3:18)**. Again, **"It is by grace you have been saved, through faith ..." (Eph. 2:8)**. And again, **"We, too, have put our faith in Christ Jesus that we may be justified by faith in Christ" (Gal. 2:16)**. Saving faith, or the lack of it, determines a person's eternal destiny and so to treat the subject lightly would be the height of folly. A clear understanding of faith is essential to this lesson.

It is well to make a clear distinction between "saving faith" and "living faith." The Bible verses cited above refer to saving faith. Saving faith is the relationship with God which the Holy Spirit bestows through the means of grace—the Word and the sacraments. The individual has nothing at all to do in obtaining saving faith; it is entirely the gift of God. That is one reason why even infants can have saving faith even though they cannot speak about knowledge, assent, and inner conscious trust in Jesus.

Living faith is also a gift of the Spirit, but it is the Christian's response to the saving faith in the grace of God that has already been bestowed by the Spirit through the Gospel. It consists of knowledge, assent (belief), and trust.

Because it is so easy to confuse living faith with saving faith, thus making salvation dependent on an attitude or work within the human being, you would do well to prepare for this lesson by reviewing "The Application of Salvation" in Francis Pieper's, *Christian Dogmatics*, vol. 2, pp. 397–557 (St. Louis: Concordia, 1951).

The Object of Faith

The object of faith is that in which one places trust. There are many who have a deep and sincere faith—even to the point of being willing to sacrifice their lives for it—but all to no avail because they have put their trust in the wrong object. The followers of Islam, proponents of communism, and devout Mormons, to mention a few, have a misplaced trust regardless of their sincerity.

That the Law can never be the object of faith is clear from **Gal. 3:12, "The law is not based on faith...."** Those who put their trust in their ability to satisfy the demands of the Law are bound to be disappointed because **"There is not a righteous man on earth who does what is right and never sins" (Eccl. 7:20)**.

Jesus made it plain that the only object of saving faith is the Gospel when He said, **"The kingdom of God is near. Repent and believe the good news!" (Mark 1:15)**. Faith based on anything less than God's promise of grace in Christ Jesus is not a saving faith. **"Whoever believes in the Son has eternal life, but whoever rejects the Son will not see life, for God's wrath remains on him" (John 3:36)**.

The Functions of Faith

Like fire, which produces both heat and light, faith has two functions (purposes). St. Paul mentions the first purpose in **Rom. 3:28, "A man is justified by faith apart from observing the law."** Through the faith given by the Spirit through the Word, the sinner receives the full and free forgiveness earned by the atoning death of Jesus Christ. He now stands before God completely acquitted and under no threat of condemnation. And so the first function of faith is justification.

But faith also has a second function. Saving faith produces a renewal of the heart which results in a different manner of life (living faith). We might also call this the sanctifying function of faith. It is to this function that St. Paul refers in **Gal. 2:20, "The life I live in the body, I live by faith in the Son of God, who loved me and gave Himself for me."** And again in **Gal. 5:6, "For in Christ Jesus neither circumcision nor uncircumcision has any value. The only thing that counts is faith expressing itself through love."** The Lutheran Confessions affirm "that good works, like fruits of a good tree, certainly and indubitably follow genuine faith—if it is a living and not a dead faith" (FC Ep V 6).

INTRODUCTION

Use this section to introduce the lesson. You may want to share other stories that illustrate faith.

SEEING THE INVISIBLE (Objectives 1 and 2)

Many young Christians are embarrassed because so much of what we believe is based on a blind trust with little empirical proof. Yet much of what passes for science is really based on faith; scientists deal with hypotheses and probabilities. For our faith we have the testimony of the Spirit of God Himself.

THE FAITH HALL OF FAME (Objectives 3 and 4)

This portion of the period is to be given to reports by the students. About halfway thought the reports you may want to take a break by reading through **Heb. 11:13–16** with the class. This section emphasizes the unproven nature of faith and is not covered in any of the student reports.

TOO NUMEROUS TO MENTION (Objective 5)

There are obviously many other heroes who could be mentioned. The Bible characters to whom reference might be made include the following:

1. Women received back their dead: the widow of Zarephath **(1 Kings 17:17–24)** or the Shunammite **(2 Kings 4:18–37)**.

2. Tortured and refused release: Jeremiah (**Jer. 20:1–2**) or the Maccabean patriots (**2 Macc. 7**).
3. Jeers and flogging: Jeremiah and other prophets.
4. Chains and prison: Joseph (**Gen. 39:20**) or Micaiah (**1 Kings 22:27**).
5. Stoned: Zechariah (**2 Chron. 24:20–21**).
6. Sawed in two: Isaiah, according to tradition.
7. Death by sword: Many prophets (**1 Kings 19:10**).

If time permits, reference may also be made to the many martyrs of the early Christian Church. Students might be asked to tell of people whom they have known who might be classified as heroes of the faith.

WHY GOD WAITED (Objective 6)

Ask students to mention some of the promises of God which we have seen fulfilled, but which the Old Testament heroes never lived to see. Especially note the historic coming of Jesus, who lived, died, and rose from the grave for us. What are some of God's promises that we have not yet seen fulfilled? The passage in **2 Peter 3:8–9** makes it clear that God is waiting so that more people may come to faith.

12. The Race to Mount Zion

CENTRAL TRUTH

The church is strengthened for the endurance race to heaven by the example of Christ, the training discipline of the Father, and the anticipation of the glorious trophy assured to all who reach the finish line in faith.

OBJECTIVES

That the students by the power of the Spirit will

1. identify worldly influences which may harm the Christian's faith;
2. reaffirm a willingness to take up their crosses and follow Jesus;
3. recognize the love and wisdom of God demonstrated in His disciplining of His children;
4. rejoice in the righteousness and peace which is theirs through the Gospel;
5. acknowledge the responsibility of Christians to strengthen the weak in faith;
6. recognize the need at times to exclude godless persons from Christian fellowship with the aim of eventual restoration to the fellowship of God's people; and
7. trust solely in the grace of God in Jesus Christ for eternal life with Him.

BACKGROUND

Punishment, Chastisement, and Cross

Because many terms are used interchangeably to discuss the troubles that occur in the lives of people, we may become confused as we speak of difficulties as experienced by Christians. We do well to distinguish among three different concepts as used to describe difficulties in the lives of people.

1. *Punishment* can be regarded as being God's judgment on impenitent sinners which they themselves bring upon themselves through their unbelief and persistence in willful sinning in spite of God's offer of forgiveness and a new life. Because Christians have been fully forgiven in Jesus Christ, whatever difficulties they experience are not punishment for sin. As St. Paul asserted, "**Therefore, there is now no condemnation for those who are in Christ Jesus,**" (Rom. 8:1). "**Who will bring any charge against those whom God has chosen? It is God who justifies**" (**Rom. 8:33**).

2. *Chastisement* might be regarded as the difficulties that God permits Christians to experience. The purpose of these trials is not to punish Christians for their sins, but to lead ("discipline") them into a closer walk with their Lord.

3. A *cross* might be regarded as those difficulties that befall Christians as a result of their faithful discipleship to Jesus Christ and courageous witness to His Word. Jesus had this in mind when He said, "**Blessed are you when people insult you, persecute you and falsely say all kinds of evil against you because of Me**" (**Matt. 5:11**) He cautioned His disciples in **Matt. 16:24–25, "If anyone would come after Me, he must deny himself and take up his cross and follow Me. For whoever wants to save his life will lose it, but whoever loses his life for Me will find it."**

Judging Other People

Perhaps no other passage of Scripture is more frequently quoted out of context and misused than **Matt. 7:1, "Do not judge, or you too will be judged."** This statement of Jesus does not mean that we Christians are never to evaluate the behavior of others. For example, Jesus encouraged his hearers to listen to the Pharisees whenever they taught them from the books of Moses, but not to follow the example of their hypocritical lives (**Matt. 23:1–12**).

Many times in Scripture God's people are urged to use God's Word to evaluate the message of those who claim to speak for God. Often in Scripture, such as in **Heb. 12:14–17** or **1 Cor. 5**, Christians are told to admonish, discipline, or correct one another.

What Scripture does warn against is our trying to play God. We all are sinful human beings. Although we may avoid certain sins, we sin in other ways. We all alike are sinners before God and live only under His forgiveness. When we do counsel one another, we are to do so in the awareness of our own sin (e.g., **Rom.**

2:1–11), in the recognition that only God is the judge of all people, and in the sincere desire to help the person whom we counsel.

Mount Zion

Mount Zion was one of the hills on which Jerusalem stood. It was a Jebusite fortress captured by David and renamed the city of David. The ark of the covenant was brought there and remained until it was moved to the temple of Solomon on Mount Moriah. From that time on the word "Zion" came to refer to the temple itself. Gradually Mount Zion came to mean the entire city of Jerusalem. In the New Testament, Zion sometimes refers to heaven as in **Heb. 12:22** and **Rev. 14:1**.

INTRODUCTION

In this lesson the writer likens the Christian life to a race. In **1 Cor. 9:24–27** and several other places, St. Paul uses a similar picture. You might introduce the lesson by discussing the topic of racing. To be sure that the outline is clear to students, you might write on the chalkboard: Preparing—Training—Running—the Finish.

ON YOUR MARK (Objectives 1 and 2)

Encourage students to share ideas about worldly entanglements which must be discarded for effective Christian running. The main emphasis is to be on the example of Jesus. No better advice can be given to young Christians than that they always ask, "What would Jesus say or do in this situation?" Involve the students in an analysis of Jesus' running style.

GET SET (Objectives 3, 4, and 5)

Straining against what they perceive to be the shackles of discipline, your students are likely to "get into" this topic. By now they have heard all of the cliches, like, "We're only doing this because we love you," . . . "It's for your own good," . . . and "Someday you'll look back and thank us." Ask them to imagine what they would be like today if their parents had never disciplined them. Explore with them that which motivates a person to discipline another.

Let students share experiences when they felt that they had been disciplined. Lead them to accept, and even rejoice in, the discipline of God.

In **Matt. 5:11–12** Jesus urges us not only to endure crosses but to **"rejoice and be glad, because great is your reward in heaven."** The gain is obviously worth the pain. According to **Luke 14:27,** the alternative is to be excluded from discipleship, with the resulting loss of the heavenly reward.

Be sure that students do not miss the beautiful point that is made at the end of this section. Stronger, better-trained Christians are to use their abilities to help the "lame" or weaker brothers and sisters so that they will not drop out of the race.

GO! (Objective 4 and 6)

This section may cause some difficulties because it instructs us to make judgments about the conduct of others. Use the information in the background section to explore this topic with the class. Church discipline is not very popular in our day, but the Bible makes it clear that those who obstruct the path of others must be removed from the track. Emphasize that the purpose of church discipline is to lead people who are unrepentant to understand their spiritual danger and to accept the forgiveness and new life Jesus offers them.

THE SPRINT TO ZION (Objective 5 and 7)

This is an opportunity to call attention to the difference between a Law-oriented theology and an evangelical faith. Here we are encouraged to trust not in ourselves but solely in the grace of God and His saving work in our behalf in the life, death, and resurrection of Jesus Christ.

13. Faith Responds to God's Love

CENTRAL TRUTH

Through the Gospel the sinner is not only justified for the sake of the substitutionary life, suffering, and death of Jesus Christ, but the Holy Spirit also produces within the believer a rich harvest of godly behavior.

OBJECTIVES

That the students by the power of the Spirit will

1. explain the cause/effect relationship between justification and sanctification;
2. demonstrate love for God by an unselfish love for other people;
3. recognize the need to keep the desire for material things in the proper perspective;
4. experience the joy of sanctified living;
5. reaffirm a determination to remain faithful to the Gospel of Christ.

INTRODUCTION

This lesson deals with the good works which a Christian inevitably performs in response to God's gracious love in Christ Jesus. You might begin by calling attention to how students demonstrate who they are. For example, a football player may wear a letter jacket to proclaim to the world that he is a football player. Others may wear some emblem to denote membership in the band, the choir, or some other organization.

Point out that it is not the wearing of the symbol that makes one a member of the group. Perhaps you could ask a petite girl to put on a football jacket and ask if that makes her a football player. Explain that good works are similar in the lives of Christians. They do not make one a Christian (there are many atheists who live moral lives); however, believers are eager to do good in response to God's saving love and work through Jesus Christ. Emphasize that for the Christian good works are not any more optional than is the wearing of a football uniform by players during a game. **"Faith without deeds is dead" (James 2:26).**

As you read through the introductory paragraphs with the class, take some time to study the **Micah** passage which shows that already in the Old Testament God had made it clear that believers will respond to His saving love through a life of goodness.

GRATEFUL WORSHIP (Objectives 1 and 4)

Remind students of the comparison of Sinai and Zion in the last lesson. The writer uses this comparison to introduce a new topic. Ask students to suggest practical ways in which Paul's instructions in **Rom. 12:1–2** can be carried out in their lives.

THE BOTTOM LINE IS LOVE
(Objectives 2 and 3)

Whenever students and all other Christians face a specific situation which involves a moral decision, the great question to ask is, "In what way would this action demonstrate love to God and love to my neighbor?" Stress the joy in being a member of an extended family of fellow Christians, with whom we share our joys and provide mutual support as we seek to overcome our weaknesses. Ask for examples of ways in which congregations might foster, or fail to foster, such a family feeling among their members.

Don't let this turn into a gripe session. Keep it positive by concentrating on what each of us can do to contribute to a family atmosphere. If time permits, look up the passages cited, or assign them to be paraphrased. Ask if any student can remember an Old Testament story when someone "entertained angels without knowing it" **(Gen. 18, Judg. 6, Judg. 13).** Perhaps students can recall a time when they were put down or placed in an embarrassing position because they defended another person.

Make the points about marriage by studying together **Eph. 5:21–33,** but don't allow this topic to dominate the lesson. The subject of submission of wives could easily take a week! However, note that the section begins with **verse 21** which stresses that we all are to be subject to one another—wives to their husbands and husbands to their wives. Paul then continues to describe how such mutual subjection is to be carried out.

Also note that the Greek word for "subjection" suggests a cooperative spirit and relationship, that each can fulfill his or her responsibilities in the Christian home. Students should also understand that the attitude one has toward one's spouse is indicative of the person's relationship with God.

The subject of the love of money is another one that cannot be dealt with at length right now. Make the necessary points and move on.

We are living in a day when honor and respect for the ministers of the Gospel needs to be reinforced among young people. This is an opportunity for presenting to students the opportunities for services offered by full-time ministry in the church. Share with the class your personal joy in having the opportunity to share the Word with others.

WARNING: KEEP OUT (Objective 5)

Here is another opportunity to stress that it is the Gospel, not the Law, that offers the way of salvation. The function of the Law is to bring us to the realization that we are indeed sinners before God, that we are unable to save ourselves, and that we need the Savior. Remind students that all people have a natural knowledge of the Law, but that the Gospel is "folly" to so many people **(1 Cor. 2:14).** On the other hand, what may make good sense to most people may be "strange" and foreign to the Christian's thinking.

THEREFORE . . . (Objectives 1 and 4)

Have students suggest fill-ins for the blanks in the first paragraph. For example: diligent studying—I got a good grade; asking six different girls—I got a date for homecoming; astigmatism—I wear glasses, etc. Make sure that students understand what is meant by a cause/effect relationship. Explain that it is not always easy to distinguish cause and effect such as in the case of a popular boy who is also very self-confident. Is he popular because he's self-confident, or is he self-confident because he's popular?

Apply this discussion to faith and good works. The one produces the other, but we must always be careful when dealing with others because it is not always easy to distinguish cause and effect. In the case of a hypocrite, the cause of good behavior is something other than faith. Also, a very weak believer may appear to be producing very little fruit. The important thing for each of us is to use this idea to evaluate our own behavior—not to put down others.

A CLOSING BENEDICTION (Objective 5)

Compare the closing benediction in **Heb. 13:20–25** with the endings of some of the other New Testament epistles. You might have students write a personal benediction for some other member of the class and exchange them.

AN ANNOUNCEMENT

Inform the class that the next session will be devoted to a review of the letter to the **Hebrews** and that the session after that will be given to the first major test.

14. The Letter to the Hebrews: A Review

The comprehensive review presented in the Student book is related specifically to the test on **Hebrews** provided for use in session 15 of this guide. Request that students look over this review session before class, and be prepared to identify those items that are unclear to them. To accomplish this review in one session you will need to keep things moving. Spend extra time only on those items with which students seem to be having problems.

DEFINITIONS

Prophet: one who brings messages from God to people.

Priest: one who fulfills legal requirements, offers sacrifices, and intercedes in behalf of people before God.

King: one who is recognized as an authoritative leader.

Melchizedek: an Old Testament priest who was a symbol or type of Christ.

Covenant: an agreement involving two or more parties. May be negotiated between two or more parties, or it may be established unilaterally. May or may not require some contribution from each party.

Testament: another word for covenant.

Gospel: the Good News of God's undeserved love in Christ. Everything God has done, and continues to do, in Christ for our salvation.

Law: that Word of God which shows people their sinfulness and is intended to bring the sinner to repentance and a realization of their need for God's free forgiveness. Everything that we are to do and not to do; how we are to be.

Tabernacle: the moveable tent which the Israelites used as a worship center; its use began during the wanderings in the wilderness and continued until the building of the temple by Solomon.

Antilegomena: those New Testament books which were for a time not universally accepted in the church as the inspired Word of God. These include all the books from **Hebrews** to **Revelation** except for **1 Peter** and **1 John.**

Homologoumena: those New Testament books which enjoyed universal acceptance in the early church from the beginning. All books except the antilegomena.

Moses: the most admired and respected of the Old Testament leaders. Led the people from slavery in Egypt to the Promised Land. The father of ancient Israel who gave the people their constitution in the five books of Moses.

Justification: God's verdict on the sinner of not guilty for the sake of the substitutionary life, sufferings, death, and resurrection of Jesus Christ. Forgiveness. Acquittal. "Just as if I never sinned."

Sanctification: the Gospel-motivated and Spirit-led life of good works which the believer follows as a result of conversion (fruit of God's free gift of justification).

Cross: earthly trouble in the life of a Christian as a result of faithfulness to Christ. May take the form of persecution or self-denial.

Discipline: earthly trouble which God permits to happen in a Christian's life as a result of our sinful nature. It is motivated by God's love and is intended for correction and improvement—never as punishment because of His wrath.

Reconciliation: the peaceful relationship between God and man established by Jesus Christ through His atoning sacrifice for sin, which made us at one with God.

Faith: confident trust in what one knows to be true, but cannot prove by tangible evidence.

Mount Zion: the hill in Jerusalem on which David established the center of Israelite worship. Later the term came to refer to the temple or to the entire city. In the New Testament it is used as a figurative expression for heaven.

Mount Sinai: the mountain on which God gave the Law to Moses after the deliverance from Egyptian slavery. In **Hebrews** it represents the Old Covenant or the Law.

Sacrifice: an offering by people either to appease God's wrath or to express gratitude for His blessings.

Sacrament: "a sacred act, instituted by God, in which there are certain visible means connected with His word, through which God offers, gives, and seals to us the forgiveness of sins which Christ earned for us."

General Epistle: a letter which was originally addressed to Christians in general rather than to a specific group or individual.

Inspiration: the in-breathing of the Holy Spirit by which He moved chosen "men to write, and put into their minds, the very thoughts which they expressed and the very words which they wrote."

Kingdom of grace: all true believers in Christ; the church on earth through which the saving Gospel is to be taught and proclaimed for the nurture of believers and the conversion of the heathen.

Kingdom of glory: heaven, where Christ rules over all those who have finished their earthly race and now live with Him forever.

Kingdom of power: all created things which Christ

rules and manages for the benefit of His Kingdom of Grace.

Joshua: the successor to Moses as the leader of Israel who finally led the Israelites into the promised land. He is referred to in **Hebrews** as a type of Christ who leads His people to heaven.

DISCUSSION QUESTIONS

1. Probably Jewish Christians living in the city of Rome. The reference in **13:24** to "those from Italy" may be cited as evidence.

2. The writer, though unknown, was certainly a man of Jewish ancestry who had not been a close associate of Jesus during His earthly ministry.

3. The main purpose of the book is to encourage Christians to remain faithful to the Gospel, and to resist any temptation to return to a reliance on the Law for their salvation.

4. The book was probably written shortly after the beginning of Nero's persecution in A.D. 64. Persecutions had obviously begun, but the many references to temple worship indicate that the temple was still standing.

5. In view of the discussion about antilegomena and homologoumena, it is important to emphasize the fact that all canonical books of the Bible are the Word of God and are authoritative for the Christian.

6. The Bible is the only completely reliable source of information about God available to Christians today through which the Holy Spirit accomplishes His saving work.

7. The Gospel is the only proper motivation for good works. The sanctified lives of Christians are their grateful response to what God gives and accomplishes in them in Jesus Christ.

8. God's justice is His fairness according to which our debt of sin must be paid in full. God's demand for the satisfaction of His justice led Jesus to the cross in order to settle our account with His Father. To satisfy God's justice, Jesus during His lifetime perfectly fulfilled every demand of God's law in our behalf (active obedience). He also endured God's judgment and condemnation for our sin through His substitutionary suffering and death (passive obedience).

9. God's grace is His undeserved love for all people. It is His gracious love that moved Him to offer His own Son for the sins of people.

10. Review the design of the tabernacle as presented in session 7. Note the similarities between the tabernacle design and churches of today, e.g., the curtain and the altar rail, the laver and the font, the ark and the altar, the levels of approach to God, the courtyard and the nave, etc. Be sure that students note especially the opening in the altar rail which symbolizes the direct access which Christians enjoy to God, but which was denied the Old Testament people.

11. Various responses may be expected. The main point to make is that the book is very relevant for young Christians.

12. Jesus as the "Word" clearly established His prophetic office as the One who reveals God to people directly. Not only His spoken words, but everything about Him speaks a message from God.

13. Christ functioned, and continues to function, as prophet by revealing God to people. While He lived on earth He did this directly; now He does it through the inspired Scriptures. His priestly function was to keep the Law perfectly for us, to offer Himself as the final sacrifice for sin, and to intercede for us with the Father. The only priestly role He now fills is as our mediator with the Father, since His one-time sacrifice for sin eliminated the need for further sacrifice. He continues to rule as King over the kingdoms of grace, power, and glory.

14. A major portion of **Hebrews** deals with this question. The basic difference is that the Old Covenant was that of the promises and the New Covenant is that of the fulfillment of the promises in Jesus of Nazareth, the Savior of all people.

15. God through the Bible clearly encourages Christians to join with others for mutual edification, for admonition in time of weakness, for spurring on in time of laxity, for comfort in sorrow, and for strengthening in times of temptation.

16. The unforgivable sin against the Holy Spirit is the deliberate and willful rejection of the converting activity of the Spirit in spite of better knowledge.

17. Courage in time of persecution can be found in remembering past victories, concentrating on the ultimate prize of heaven, and relying on God's promise that He will never permit more than we can bear.

18. Comfort in time of discipline comes from the knowledge that in His relationships with believers God is motivated by fatherly love and caring concern for their welfare—never by anger and a desire for vengeance.

19. At times the Christian community may out of love and concern for the unrepentant sinner remove that person from their fellowship (excommunication) to lead that person to recognize the seriousness of his or her situation before God, to repent, and to be restored in faith through the Gospel.

20. The Old Testament sacrifices pointed to the Christ who by His perfect sacrifice would atone for the sin of all humanity from the beginning of time to the end.

21. The book of **Hebrews** especially warns against sexual immorality, trust in earthly riches, failure to honor and respect faithful leaders in the church, and the human tendency to rely on one's own righteousness for salvation.

22. The problems of the adolescent church which are faced by young people today include the questioning of the traditional values of childhood, the loosening of parental (apostolic) control, and the allurements of the society in which they live.

23. Quickly review the names discussed in session 11.

24. Because we have been justified freely by God's grace in Christ, we respond with a sanctified life. We do not live godly lives in order to be forgiven; we serve and obey God because we have been forgiven.

25. In Scripture angels function in several capacities, but the work of bringing messages from God to people is the one emphasized in **Hebrews.**

15. Test: The Letter to the Hebrews

Name _____ Hour _____

TRUE/FALSE

Decide which of the following statements are true and which are false. If a statement is true, put a plus sign (+) on the line provided. If it is false, put a zero (0).

___ 1. The last books of the New Testament to be written should be taken more seriously by Christians than the earlier ones.

___ 2. The last books of the New Testament have always been universally accepted by the Christian church.

___ 3. The letter to the Hebrews was probably addressed to Christians living in the city of Rome.

___ 4. The main purpose of this letter was to instruct Jewish Christians in the proper way to live in accordance to God's laws.

___ 5. This letter is not very relevant for today's youth, but will be important to them later in life.

___ 6. The main function of a prophet in the Bible was to deliver messages from God to people.

___ 7. In the Bible Jesus is sometimes referred to as "the Word."

___ 8. The only completely clear and reliable message from God is to be found in the Bible.

___ 9. Most Jews considered Moses to be the greatest leader of the Old Testament.

___ 10. Christians should obey Jesus mostly because they have to.

___ 11. As long as people believe in Him, God doesn't mind too much if they disobey Him once in a while.

___ 12. The main function of the Old Testament priests was to proclaim God's Word to people.

___ 13. Jesus finished His work as our Priest when He offered Himself on the cross as the sacrifice for our sins.

___ 14. Melchizedek was an Old Testament priest who symbolized the work of Christ.

___ 15. The Old Covenant was a failure because it was a bad idea in the first place.

___ 16. In the Bible the words "covenant" and "testament" mean the same thing.

___ 17. The "New Covenant" offers God's forgiveness unconditionally.

___ 18. There are many similarities between the design of the Old Testament tabernacle and our church buildings of today.

___ 19. The open altar rail in our churches symbolizes that we are still separated from God by our sins.

___ 20. In the Old Testament the high priest entered the "most holy place" (Holy of Holies) once each week to represent the people before God.

___ 21. Because He loves us, God does not demand payment for our sins.

___ 22. The blood of Jesus cleans people on the inside as well as the outside.

___ 23. Jesus' sacrifice for sin is repeated each time we celebrate the Lord's Supper.

___ 24. It is very important for Christians to join with fellow believers in a local congregation.

___ 25. Deliberate and willful sinning may place one's eternal salvation in jeopardy.

___ 26. There is little to be gained by remembering your faith experiences of the past.

___ 27. Faith is not based upon visible proof of what it believes.

___ 28. Faith is not just wishful thinking, but sure and solid confidence.

___ 29. Many of the Old Testament heroes of the faith never lived to see the final fulfillment of God's promises to them.

___ 30. We should never make judgments about behavior of other Christians.

___ 31. When God allows sorrow to come into our lives, it is only because of His anger over our sinfulness.

___ 32. In this letter Mount Zion represents the Gospel and Mount Sinai represents the Law.

___ 33. In the Old Testament God forgave the people's sins because they sacrificed animals to Him as required.

___ 34. A wealthy Christian faces fewer temptations than one who is poor.

___ 35. A life of good works does not necessarily prove that a person is a Christian.

MULTIPLE CHOICE

Choose the BEST ending for each of the following statements and print the letter of your choice on the line provided.

___ 36. Those New Testament books which were almost immediately accepted as canonical by all Christians are called
A. general.
B. homologoumena.
C. antilegomena.
D. inspired.

___ 37. Those New Testament books which are not addressed to any specific person or group are said to be
A. gospels.
B. antilegomena.
C. homologoumena.
D. general.

___ 38. A special problem of the adolescent church was

A. the lack of missionary zeal.
B. the death and aging of the Apostles.
C. translating the Old Testament into Greek.
D. all of the above.

___ 39. The writer of Hebrews was probably
A. St. Paul.
B. Timothy.
C. a Jewish person who had been a close friend of Jesus.
D. a Jewish person who had not known Jesus personally.

___ 40. The spiritual decisions made by a young adult are
A. not usually important in the long run.
B. very important for one's future spiritual life.
C. usually only temporary.
D. almost always wrong.

___ 41. Hebrews was probably written
A. shortly after the destruction of Jerusalem in A.D. 70.
B. shortly before the destruction of Jerusalem in A.D. 70.
C. before the beginning of any persecution of Christians.
D. right after Pentecost.

___ 42. Scientific investigation is a good source of information about
A. the creation of the world.
B. what happens to people after they die.
C. what combination of foods provides the best nutrition.
D. how to deal with a severe guilt complex.

___ 43. Jesus is a better spokesperson for God than angels because
A. the angels are obedient to Him.
B. He is without sin.
C. He is a spirit without a human body.
D. all of the above.

___ 44. Jesus functioned as God's messenger to people
A. only when he spoke the words printed in red in some Bibles
B. by all of His words and actions.
C. by His words, but not always by His actions.
D. only after he came into the world as a human being.

___ 45. Christ's Kingdom of grace consists of
A. heaven.
B. all the Christians
C. the entire universe.
D. all angels.

___ 46. The Gospel brings joy to our hearts because
A. it frees us from the need to obey God.
B. it promises that we will be free of all earthly sorrow.
C. it assures us of life and salvation.
D. all of the above.

___ 47. The Old Testament leader Joshua symbolized Jesus because
A. his father was also a carpenter.
B. the people obeyed him perfectly.
C. he led the people into a promised land.
D. he was anointed by God.

___ 48. When it comes to religious knowledge, Christians should
A. progress beyond the basics to the more mature issues.
B. stay childlike and be content with the basics.
C. get into religious arguments whenever possible to sharpen their thinking.
D. believe whatever church leaders tell them.

___ 49. Jesus serves as our High Priest today by
A. giving us pastors to preach the Word of God to us.
B. interceding for us before His Father's throne.
C. offering Himself in the Eucharist for the sins of all people.
D. ruling the universe for the benefit of His believers.

___ 50. Because of Jesus' reconciling death on the cross each of us
A. is a spiritually blind, dead enemy of God.
B. is a royal priest.
C. should become a pastor.
D. must do good works to pay for our sins.

___ 51. An agreement between two parties is called
A. a covenant.
B. a tabernacle.
C. a reconciliation.
D. an ordinance.

___ 52. The book of Hebrews points to Jesus' way as the best
A. because He offers an eternal covenant.
B. because he intercedes for us before the Father.
C. because He is the only savior for all people.
D. all of the above.

___ 53. A covenant
A. always requires a contribution from each party.
B. is always negotiated between two equal parties.
C. always offers some benefit to each party.
D. is sometimes established by one party for the benefit of the other.

___ 54. In the Old Testament all the people were allowed
A. into the Most Holy Place of the tabernacle.
B. into the Holy Place of the tabernacle.
C. to make offerings on the altar of incense.
D. into the courtyard of the tabernacle.

___ 55. In the Old Testament the curtain separated
A. the courtyard from the Holy Place.
B. the ark of the covenant from the Most Holy Place.
C. the tabernacle from the courtyard.

D. the Most Holy Place from the Holy Place.

___ 56. To show that people were reconciled to God when Jesus died
   A. an earthquake shook the ground.
   B. there was darkness all around.
   C. the veil in the temple was torn in two.
   D. the soldiers cast lots for His clothes.

___ 57. Jesus died because
   A. He was a true human being.
   B. He chose to.
   C. He had no alternative.
   D. the soldiers overpowered Him.

___ 58. God demanded the death of Jesus to pay for sin
   A. To satisfy His justice.
   B. To show His mercy and grace to lost sinners.
   C. To gain eternal life for His people.
   D. All of the above.

___ 59. The Hebrews were asked to remember the persecutions they had successfully endured in order to
   A. give them confidence in their present temptations.
   B. frighten them into compliance with God's laws.
   C. encourage them to keep up the ancient Hebrew traditions.
   D. all of the above.

___ 60. It is easier to face suffering in this world if
   A. we are supported by other Christians.
   B. we keep remembering the reward which will be ours in heaven.
   C. we focus on the suffering of Jesus on our behalf.
   D. all of the above.

___ 61. Christians are motivated to live a godly life by
   A. the hope of earthly happiness.
   B. the threats of the Law.
   C. the good news of the Gospel.
   D. none of the above.

___ 62. As an example of a hero of the faith, the writer to the Hebrews mentions
   A. Adam.
   B. Solomon.
   C. Joseph.
   D. all of the above.

___ 63. God is still waiting to keep some of His promises because
   A. He is giving more people time to come to faith.
   B. He wants to put Christians through more testing.
   C. Satan is not quite defeated yet.
   D. all of the above.

___ 64. The best example for us in the race of life is
   A. one of the faith heroes of the past.
   B. Martin Luther.
   C. one of our parents.
   D. Jesus.

___ 65. God's greatest demonstration of His tough love was
   A. His destruction of the world by a flood.
   B. His drowning of the Egyptian army in the Red Sea.
   C. His punishment of Jesus on the the cross.
   D. the destruction of Jerusalem in A.D. 70.

___ 66. God's discipline is always
   A. motivated by His love.
   B. in the best interest of the person beings disciplined.
   C. without error.
   D. all of the above.

___ 67. In the race toward heaven
   A. it's every man for himself.
   B. we are in competition with other people.
   C. Christians are to help those who are having difficulty.
   D. all of the above.

___ 68. The Old Testament offerings were actually
   A. sacrifices.
   B. optional.
   C. rites pointing to the Christ and His sacrifice.
   D. contrary to God's will.

___ 69. The one word that best describes a God-pleasing life is
   A. love.
   B. happiness.
   C. patience.
   D. hope.

___ 70. Faith and good works are related to each other in this way:
   A. good works are the inevitable result of faith.
   B. good works always produce faith.
   C. faith sometimes produces good works.
   D. good works sometimes produce faith.

71–75. Choose a passage from the book of Hebrews which, in your opinion, summarizes the main them of the letter. Write out the passage in the space below. Explain the passage and tell why you chose it.

Answer Key: Test on Hebrews

TRUE/FALSE

1. 0	13. 0	25. +
2. 0	14. +	26. 0
3. +	15. 0	27. +
4. 0	16. +	28. +
5. 0	17. +	29. +
6. +	18. +	30. 0
7. +	19. 0	31. 0
8. +	20. 0	32. +
9. +	21. 0	33. 0
10. 0	22. +	34. 0
11. 0	23. 0	35. +
12. 0	24. +	

MULTIPLE CHOICE

36. B	48. A	60. D
37. D	49. B	61. C
38. B	50. B	62. C
39. D	51. A	63. A
40. B	52. D	64. D
41. B	53. D	65. C
42. C	54. D	66. D
43. A	55. D	67. C
44. B	56. C	68. C
45. B	57. B	69. A
46. C	58. D	70. A
47. C	59. A	

CHAPTER 2
THE LETTER OF JAMES

16. Living the Faith

CENTRAL TRUTH

James, the first of the so-called "general" epistles, is an early call to Christians, wherever they may be, to examine their daily conduct in the light of God's Law. It gives us the understanding that sincere faith in Jesus will inevitably produce the fruit of good works.

OBJECTIVES

That the students by the power of the Spirit will

1. define the term "general epistle" and list the New Testament books which are included in this classification;
2. demonstrate an understanding of the cause and effect relationship between faith and works;
3. identify the writer of **James** and relate the significant facts of his life as we know them;
4. identify the recipients of this epistle and describe their life situation;
5. indicate the probable date of the letter and explain the reasons for that conclusion;
6. recognize the poetic form and style of the letter;
7. rejoice in the free gift of salvation and pray for the help of the Holy Spirit in living a God-pleasing life.

BACKGROUND

The text refers to Hebrew poetic parallelism, a literary feature that is prominent in the letter of **James.** Some understanding of this feature helps us to appreciate Hebrew poetry and, at times, to interpret specific Bible passages more accurately. At this point a very brief description of this literary device is helpful.

A parallelism is a literary form in which thoughts are expressed in two-line sections, with the second line closely related to the first. In the simplest type, synonymous parallelism, the second line repeats the thought of the first but in different words. **Ps. 2:1** is a clear example.

> "Why do the nations conspire
> and the peoples plot in vain?"

Ps. 107:35 is another.

> "He turned the desert into pools of water
> and the parched ground into flowing springs."

Another form, antithetic parallelism, occurs when the second line expresses a thought opposite that in the first line. **Ps. 1:6** is an example.

> "For the Lord watches over the way of the righteous,
> but the way of the wicked will perish."

Prov. 12:22 is another example of the antithetic type.

> "The Lord detests lying lips,
> but He delights in men who are truthful."

As can be seen in the following examples, **James** is rich in this form of poetry.

> "The brother in humble circumstances ought
>   to take pride in his high position.
> But the one who is rich should take pride in
>   his low position." (1:9–10a)

> "You see that his faith and his actions were
>   working together,
> and his faith was made complete by what he
>   did." (2:22)

In all, there are at least six different types of parallelisms, but these two provide basic examples.

THE GENERAL EPISTLES (Objective 1)

This section introduces the second major unit of this course: The General Epistles. Although students were introduced to recipients of these books in the first session of this course, a brief review is in order. Ask students to scan quickly the opening verses of the books and note the addressees.

James—Christians of the "twelve tribes of Israel," probably Jewish Christians, or it may mean all Christians who are now the "new Israel."

1 Peter—Christians throughout Asia Minor.

2 Peter—Possibly a second letter to those who received the first letter. One minority view (e.g., Zahn) is that of Jewish Christians throughout Palestine.

1 John—No reference at all to the possible addressee.

2 John—"Elect lady and her children" seems to allude to the Christians in a specific congregation.

3 John—Gaius, a commonly held name in the first century, is an unknown individual.

Jude—"Those who have been called, who are loved by God the Father and kept by Jesus Christ" could be any Greek-speaking Christian community; possibly some group of churches in which Jude was especially interested.

JAMES—LIVING THE FAITH (Objective 2)

Read through this section with the class and be certain that students understand that good works are not a price paid to earn God's forgiveness, but that they are a grateful response to God's free gifts. This relationship has been discussed earlier in this course, and you may begin to feel that this is needless repetition. Yet this continues to be widely misunderstood even among lifelong Christians, and needs to be constantly reinforced.

THE WRITER OF THE LETTER (Objective 3)

Ask students to discover facts about James through the study of 10 Bible passages. You may choose to work through those passages with the entire class, or you may divide them into small work groups who will report their findings. Another possibility is to assign this activity as homework. Whichever option is chosen, the following answers can be expected:

Matt. 13:55 James was a brother of the Lord and, as the first one listed, was probably the eldest.

John 7:2–5 James at one time did not recognize Jesus as Savior.

1 Cor. 15:7 Jesus made a special appearance to James after His resurrection.

Acts 1:14 James, a brother of Jesus, was once again among the believers—perhaps as a result of Jesus' appearance to him.

Jude 1:1 James was a brother to the writer of Jude.

Gal. 1:19 James was one of the two people consulted by Paul after his conversion. This indicates James' stature in the church.

Acts 15:13ff. James clearly held a leadership position in the church.

Gal. 2:9 James was a "pillar" of the church.

Acts 21:17–19 Later on, James was the leader of the Jerusalem congregation.

Acts 12:17 Another indication of the important position held by James and the obvious honor and respect accorded to him.

THE RECIPIENTS OF THE LETTER (Objective 4)

Although **1 Peter** describes all Christians as the new Israel, the position of James in Jerusalem, as well as the decidedly Hebrew character of this epistle, suggests that the recipients were of Jewish descent. The passages in Acts indicate that the people were scattered by the persecution that followed the death of Stephen. (Note that responsible scholars disagree as to whether the recipients were only Jewish Christians or were also Gentile Christians.)

THE DATE OF THE LETTER (Objective 5)

Ask students to review the timeline presented earlier.

THE LETTER'S FORM AND STYLE (Objective 6)

As time permits, present the basic idea of Hebrew parallelism, using the information in the background section. Besides the examples given, the following passages in **James** are characteristic of **Hebrew** poetry: **1:15; 1:17; 1:19–20; 1:22–23; 4:7, 4:10.**

OPERATING INSTRUCTIONS (Objective 7)

Students will no doubt have received electronic or other devices that required a heavy reliance on operating instructions. Use this section to motivate students to read the book of **James** by the next session.

17. Brother of the Lord

CENTRAL TRUTH

The Christian ethics advocated by James bear a striking resemblance to the moral standards commanded by Jesus. These form the foundation for the sanctified life which the believer offers to God as a sacrifice of thanksgiving in response to the Gospel.

OBJECTIVES

That the students by the power of the Spirit will

1. discover the amazingly close resemblance between the thoughts and words of Jesus and James;
2. explain this similarity on the basis of their close relationship as brothers;
3. identify the ethical concepts found both in James and in the Sermon on the Mount;
4. recognize their own failure to meet these standards;
5. declare a willingness, with the help of God, to amend their sinful lives;
6. identify ways in which their lives can be changed by taking God's words seriously;
7. celebrate their freedom in the Gospel which makes godly living an expression of gratitude rather than a burdensome demand.

INTRODUCTION (Objective 2)

Begin by asking students to discuss ways in which siblings resemble each other. Mannerisms, vocabulary, speech patterns, political views, ethical beliefs, etc., may be some of the similarities mentioned. Remind students that James was the brother of Jesus, and that in this lesson we will discover the amazing correlation between the way in which these two expressed themselves.

This similarity can be explained on the basis of the Holy Spirit's inspiration of Scripture. However, the Spirit uses writers according to their human talents and abilities, life situations, writing styles, and other human aspects of their being. Hence, similarities between

James and Jesus can be explained on the basis of their early association with each other.

Have the class read through the introduction and discuss any points of interest.

THE SERMON ON THE MOUNT—JAMES' VERSION (Objectives 1 and 3–7)

The entire class period will be needed for this activity. As each topic is introduced, the class can be divided with half reading aloud the words of **James**, and the other half following with the words from **Matthew**. Encourage much discussion of the implications of these ethical standards for our lives today. Urge either public or confidential evaluation of the personal life of students on the basis of these standards. Share personal experiences of your own wherever it might be appropriate.

This class period could become completely law-oriented and moralistic unless the teacher makes frequent reference to the Christian life-style as a thank-offering to God for the free gift of forgiveness. Encourage students to see the joy in Christlike living.

If time expires before completion of the topics, the remainder may be added to the assignment for the next session.

AN ASSIGNMENT (Objectives 1, 4, 5, 6, & 7)

Expected answers are
   D **Luke 16:25**
   B **Matt. 22:39**
   E **Luke 4:25**
   A **Matt. 21:21–22**
   C **Matt. 12:33–37**

18. The Royal Law: Love

CENTRAL TRUTH

A serious commitment to the royal law, **"love your neighbor as yourself,"** can produce a life characterized by impartiality, godly wisdom, and unselfish consideration of the needs and wishes of others.

OBJECTIVES

That by the grace of God the students will

1. identify the "royal law" of James as being "love your neighbor as yourself";
2. recognize that love for others is the inevitable result of Christian discipleship;
3. express remorse over their past failures to show an impartial love for all fellow Christians;
4. pray for God's help to eliminate discrimination among members of the church;
5. share suggestions for improving interpersonal relationships in the church, home, and school;
6. explain the scriptural concept of wisdom;
7. earnestly desire to be given heavenly wisdom;
8. declare a willingness to submit to God and others;
9. identify the negative results in the Christian family of an insistence on one's own way.

INTRODUCTION (Objectives 1 and 2)

Read through the introductory paragraphs, looking up together the passages which are not quoted. An examination of **Lev. 19:9–18** will reveal a remarkable correspondence with the teachings of James.

FAVORITISM FORSAKEN (Objectives 3, 4, and 5)

Work thoroughly through this section with the class. The discussion questions are designed to stimulate an interesting sharing of experiences and suggestions. If time becomes a problem, some of the questions may be assigned as homework. Be sure to conclude on the positive note suggested at the end of the section. The teacher should not hesitate to participate with observations from the standpoint of a church professional.

WISE GUYS (Objectives 6 and 7)

In connection with the topic of wisdom from a biblical perspective you may want to spend some time with **Proverbs 1–4**. This is another activity which may be assigned as homework. Students could be asked to study the first four chapters of **Proverbs** and note some of the characteristics of wisdom mentioned there.

Encourage active student participation in a discussion of the descriptions of earthly and heavenly wisdom.

SUBMISSION TO GOD AND OTHERS (Objectives 8 and 9)

Read through this material with the class and encourage open discussion of the questions provided.

CHAPTER 3
1 PETER

19. Born Again for Hopeful Living

CENTRAL TRUTH

To offer enthusiastic hope and encouragement to Christians as they struggle with the trials and temptations of life, the apostle Peter in this letter reminds them of their election to God's family through God's grace in the Savior Jesus Christ. He also assures them of their victory over sin, death, and hell accomplished through Jesus Christ by His substitutionary life, suffering, death, and resurrection.

OBJECTIVES

That the students by the power of the Spirit will

1. describe experiences in Peter's life which qualified him to offer hope in the midst of difficulties;
2. identify crises in their personal lives which can be eased by the confident hope offered by the Holy Spirit through Peter's words;
3. summarize the historical setting in which the letter was originally written;
4. celebrate the joy of knowing that they are personally chosen by God's grace to be adopted into His family through the faith-giving activity of the Holy Spirit;
5. recognize that living in a world as strangers and foreigners does create stress for the sons and daughters of God;
6. express the desire to develop attitudes of hope as one living in the victorious Christ.

INTRODUCTION (Objectives 1 and 2)

To introduce the class to the first letter of Peter, ask students to turn to **Luke 22:31–32** and read these verses aloud. Ask students to note that, while all the disciples would be tempted, Peter in particular is about to fail his Lord by denying any knowledge of Him **(Luke 22:54–62)**. But Jesus has prayed that he will repent, and that his experience will lead him to strengthen his brothers. Point out that **1 Peter** reflects how Jesus' prayer was answered.

Use the hymn verse to introduce the subjects of hope and optimism, which are based on the solid foundation of Jesus' sacrificial and atoning life, suffering, and death in full payment for the sins of all people.

Use the introductory paragraphs to introduce the students to Peter. Be sure to look up the references and note that Peter was a man who had been through spiritual valleys, and one who had also stood on spiritual mountaintops. Few people in Scripture experienced the ups and downs of faith more than Peter.

On the basis of the last paragraph in this section, encourage students to identify those times in their lives when they could have identified with Peter with their personal lows and highs.

WHO, WHAT, WHY, WHEN, WHERE? (Objective 3)

Use this section to describe the historical setting of the book. Note that Silas accompanied Paul on his second missionary journey; he also was chosen by the Jerusalem congregation to represent them to the Gentile Christians at Antioch. The excellent Greek of this epistle leads many commentators to believe that Silas served as Peter's secretary for the writing of this epistle inasmuch as Peter was most likely not very fluent in Greek. In any case, Silas played an important role in the composition of the letter.

Help students to locate on a map those areas in which the addressees of this letter resided. (Cf. **1 Peter 1:1.**) Note that they are in the northern part of Asia Minor, an area probably not visited by Paul on his journeys. That would explain why Peter rather than Paul wrote to them. Peter in **2:10** identifies at least some of his readers as Gentiles who were not originally part of God's chosen people of Israel.

The rest of this section is self-explanatory, but important for an understanding of the original situation.

CHOSEN TO BE DIFFERENT (Objectives 4 and 5)

This section is intended to establish the dual themes of election and "strangerhood"—themes used consistently throughout the study of this epistle. To help students establish these themes firmly in their minds, encourage individuals to cite personal experiences in which they were chosen for some meaningful honor. Perhaps some are adopted children who will share the special joy that comes from being "handpicked" to be a member of a family.

Discuss with your students some ways in which Christians are different from the world, and how those differences can at times lead to stressful situations. Young Christians need to find joy in being different, and not just accept it as a necessary hassle. Encourage pride in the distinctiveness of being a daughter or son of God.

Don't overlook **1 Peter 1:2,** a beautiful summary of God's plan of salvation. In four phrases, the following aspects of God's plan are identified:

1. Before the foundation of the world, God elected

those who would be His children through faith in Jesus. It is important to stay with the positive side of the doctrine of election. The negative question of why some have not been chosen must inevitably lead to an in-depth discussion of the doctrine of election and predestination; and this aspect is not fully described in Scripture for our understanding. All we know is that if we are Christian, we are thus because of the grace of God. If we are damned, it is because we ourselves rejected the grace of God in Jesus Christ.

2. The "sanctifying work of the Spirit" in this verse refers to the entire work of bringing people to faith in Jesus Christ through the means of Word and Sacrament, and of empowering them for God-pleasing lives. This is sanctification in the wider sense.

3. "Obedience to Jesus Christ" is best understood here as conversion or coming to faith. In the New Testament "obey" often means to believe (cf. **Acts 6:7, Rom. 1:5, Rom. 6:16**). It is our response to the Gospel through which the Holy Spirit works saving faith within our hearts. Of course, having come to faith in Jesus Christ, we express this relationship through our Christian life.

4. "Sprinkling by His blood" refers to complete and full forgiveness which comes to the Christian through faith in the merits of Christ Jesus, gained through His sacrificial suffering and death on the cross.

YOUR LASTING LEGACY (Objective 4)

You have several options for guiding students through this section. The discussion questions can serve as an outline for a verse-by-verse study with the entire class. Or, you could divide your class into groups to discuss the questions. If you choose this option, appoint within each group a recorder to represent the group in a plenary discussion after the period allotted for small group discussion. A third option would be to ask students to write their individual responses to the questions, and then share their thoughts with the entire class. A fourth option would be to assign the questions as homework.

Whichever method is used, the following ideas should emerge:

1. God's mercy and undeserved love is the motivation, "without any merit or worthiness in me."

2. The resurrection of Christ guaranteed our inheritance by showing that God accepted the death of His Son as payment in full for all sins.

3. Our spiritual legacy is permanent and lasting.

4. Faith (our personal relationship with God through Jesus Christ by the power of the Spirit) is our shield as we battle our spiritual enemies. St. Paul uses similar images in **Eph. 6:16.**

5. We will fully enter into our inheritance when Christ returns in glory on the Last Day.

6. God permits us to experience trials in order to strengthen our faith. Through troubles we realize our need for God in our lives. As God helps us solve our problems, we can see how God works for our good. You may wish to compare life's troubles with the sometimes painful exercises and drills that prepare one for successful athletic competition.

7. Faith is being absolutely certain about something which cannot be proven by such ordinary means as experimentation, observation, and rational thought processes.

8. Note the present tense. We already are receiving benefits of our inheritance now while we are still here on earth.

9. We are privileged to live after the historical ministry of Jesus and have precise, eye-witness accounts of His suffering, death, and resurrection.

10. Christ's suffering and death were necessary to pay the wages of sin.

11. These **"men spoke from God as they were carried along by the Holy Spirit" (2 Peter 1:21).**

THEREFORE, LIVE AS STRANGERS (Objective 6)

For this section you may wish to use one of the four options suggested for the previous section.

1. The Christian mentally prepares for action by cultivating self-control, and by keeping his sight set steadfastly on the hope of the finish line, Christ's return in glory.

2. God has declared us to be holy like He is holy. With joy we seek to live the holy life that pleases Him. As His children, we follow the pattern of our Parent.

3. In **verses 18 and 23,** Peter again mentions the imperishable nature of our inheritance.

4. "Obeying the truth" is to be interpreted as having faith in Jesus Christ as Savior. (See the material above on **1 Peter 1:2.**)

5. Some of the positive mental attitudes suggested are self-control, hopefulness, reverent fear, and love for our brothers and sisters in Christ.

6. We are warned to avoid conformity, malice, deceit, hypocrisy, envy, and slander.

7. The spiritual food for the Christian is the Word of God.

20. Chosen to Be Used and to Live as Strangers

CENTRAL TRUTH

God chooses the Christian to play a vital, contributing role in the church as a living stone patterned after Jesus the Cornerstone. This call to imitate Christ results in an attitude in home and society of high self-esteem as a redeemed and elected child of God, and yet one of servanthood to God and our fellow human beings.

OBJECTIVES

That the students by the power of the Spirit will

1. recognize that God has elected and called them to an office of active participation in the church;
2. pattern their lives after Jesus the Cornerstone;
3. discover the meaning of Peter's living stone imagery;
4. summarize the function of Christians in the world;
5. demonstrate a humble Christian spirit;
6. share their feelings about submission to authority;
7. summarize the four basic principles of church/state relationships;
8. apply the concept of submission to daily living;
9. acknowledge authority and responsibility of husband and wife to each other in the marriage relationship.

INTRODUCTION (Objective 1)

Review briefly the main thrust of the previous session—that Christians are unique in the world in that they have been chosen to receive a fabulous spiritual inheritance. Use the opening paragraph to point out that God has chosen us for active duty in the church, and not merely to be ornaments. You might remind them of the prodigal son in Jesus' parable who received his inheritance, but then wasted it by failing to use it for the purposes of God and the good of fellow human beings.

LIVING STONES (Objectives 1, 2, 3, and 4)

As you present this material to your students, you may wish to include the hymn stanza at the beginning of the lesson. Discuss the function of stones in a wall; impress on your students the equally vital role they play in the church. Point out that problems result for a wall—or a church—if some stones are not in place.

You may use the questions in different ways, such as those suggested in previous lessons. The following thoughts are idea starters, and are not necessarily the last word.

1. Perhaps Jesus was rejected because He was too perfect. He was, after all, accused of **"making Himself equal with God." (John 5:18).** A cornerstone certainly doesn't look like the other stones. Peter simply says He was rejected by "those who do not believe" **(2:7).**

2. A major topic in the study of **Hebrews** was the universal priesthood of all believers. The main function of a priest was to mediate between God and man, but through the reconciling work of Christ each of us has direct access to God. Remind students of the opening in the altar rail at church that symbolizes that access.

3. Use the passages indicated to fashion a list similar to this: praising God, witnessing, doing good, sharing with others, monetary gifts, offering of the entire self, offering of a broken spirit and a contrite heart.

4. This is simply an exercise in how to use Bible helps. The references are **Is. 28:16, Ps. 118:22,** and **Is. 8:14.**

5. Those who have faith (believe) consider Him precious, but those who lack faith reject Him.

6. The word "disobey" here clearly means to not believe. This use of the word "obey" was discussed previously. It is a very important point, however, because another interpretation leads to a trust in one's own works for acceptance and approval by God.

7. God's chosen people are to "declare the praises" of the One who rescued them from the darkness of sin and unbelief. That the willingness to confess Christ before others is a natural result of saving faith is clear from **Rom. 10:8–10, "'The word is near you; it is in your mouth and in your heart,' that is, the word of faith we are proclaiming: That if you confess with your mouth, 'Jesus is Lord,' and believe in your heart that God raised Him from the dead, you will be saved. For it is with your heart that you believe and are justified, and it is with your mouth that you confess and are saved."** Jesus also speaks of this in **Matt. 10:32–33.**

8. God's undeserved mercy as demonstrated in Jesus Christ is His motive for electing us to salvation.

MORE LIVING AS STRANGERS

Discuss this on the basis of **1 Peter 2:11–12.**

IT'S STRANGE TO BE HUMBLE (Objectives 5, 6, 7, 8, and 9)

Emphasize that we are to rejoice at opportunities to emulate Christ through Christlike humility. Too often we treat this as a depressing responsibility.

On the basis of **1 Peter 2:13–17,** discuss the four statements here presented. These represent the Christian understanding of the believer's relationship with the government. They likely will stimulate considerable discussion, and perhaps even some unanswerable questions. The following examples will set the stage. Feel free to provide more of your own.

1. The government allows people to worship false gods, which God has forbidden. The government allows divorce for less than biblical reasons. The government allows gambling, blasphemy, and many other things which God forbids. It is not the proper position of the church as an institution to attempt to have all of its moral and ethical beliefs enacted into law and forced upon the entire society. We are to influence society through faithful teaching of the Word of God. (Christians who follow in the Calvinist tradition, such as those who belonged to the Moral Majority, tend to believe that the institutional church is to order all of society.)

2. The government forbids many adiaphora (things neither commanded nor forbidden in Scripture). For example, the government may forbid citizens to burn trash without a permit. The government may forbid parking in certain restricted areas. However, out of love and concern for others, we Christians obey such laws even though they may not be found in Scripture.

3. God has forbidden murder; therefore, the government is not to force a Christian to fight in war which the Christian may regard as unjust and hence contrary to conscience. If the occasion arises, the Christian is to refuse to obey a law that requires the breaking of one of God's Commandments.

4. God has commanded regular worship; therefore, Christians are to disobey any government which makes it a crime to worship. Because God has commanded us to aid the oppressed, many Christians during the Second World War deliberately broke the law in order to shelter innocent Jewish people.

Non-government authorities that may be mentioned by students are parents, teachers, etc. God expects honor and respect for all in authority.

The next group of questions are focused on **1 Peter 2:18–25.**

1. Membership in a labor union does not automatically imply a rebellious position, and may often be necessary. Labor unions have brought many blessings to the working people by providing a unified voice in negotiations. Examples of union excesses may be brought up in class and should be openly discussed, but avoid any blanket condemnation.

2. This is largely an opinion question. Keep the discussion centered on the joy of Christian cooperation and helpfulness.

3. Encourage quiet, reasonable and humble discussion of a perceived injustice.

4. Some commentators have concluded that few, if any, of Peter's readers were of the wealthy slave-owner class.

5. Since Peter only refers to one side of the issue, a look at Paul's fuller exposition in **Eph. 6:5–9** is important. We all, regardless of our situation in life, are to serve one another.

In the discussion of **1 Peter 3:1–7** be sure to include also Paul's similar treatment of the subject in **Eph. 5:21–6:9.** Note that submissiveness as used in Scripture does not denote a master-slave relationship. Rather, we all are to be subject to one another. Submissiveness is to so cooperate with one another that we may help each person fulfill responsibilities and attain fullest potential. Here we learn how spouses are to reflect their respective attitudes of mutual submissiveness in their relationships with each other.

1. Absolutely not. We are not superior or inferior; we are different.

2. Her husband may be led to faith in Christ as a result of her godly example.

3. A gentle and quiet spirit is the source of true beauty. Be sure that students do not conclude that **"braided hair ... the wearing of gold jewelry and fine clothes"** are here condemned. That would be to miss the point entirely.

4. They were motivated by their hope in God.

5. Obviously not! The references are to two occasions when Abraham passed Sarah off as his sister, and placed her in moral jeopardy. Sarah submitted because of her devotion to God.

6. Whoever lacks the Christian's confident hope in the merciful care of God will be fearful of many things in life, including an attitude of servanthood toward others.

7. St. Paul writes in **Eph. 5:25, "Husbands, love your wives, just as Christ loved the church and gave Himself up for her."** Encourage many examples of ways in which a husband can demonstrate unselfish love for the wife. You might point out to those who feel that God's command to wives is burdensome that His expectation of husbands is equally arduous and self-effacing.

8. Encourage students to share a number of examples.

9. This probably refers only to physical strength.

10. A family in turmoil is seldom one which is able to maintain a close relationship with God.

21. Chosen to Be Baptized

CENTRAL TRUTH

Christians can exult in their baptism as a sign that they have been chosen by God for the sake of the substitutionary life, suffering, and death of Jesus Christ for membership in His family and for the eternal inheritance in heaven. As a result of God's gracious work of salvation, Christians are motivated in the power of the Spirit to live a live of grateful submission to God's will and humble service to others.

OBJECTIVES

That the students by the power of the Spirit will

1. celebrate their baptism as evidence that they are chosen by God to be royal priests;
2. summarize the major themes previously identified in Peter's first epistle;
3. reaffirm their trust that in Baptism they received faith in Christ and the forgiveness of sins;
4. recognize the power of Baptism to motivate a daily commitment to sanctified living;
5. identify ways in which they can live as strangers in the world;
6. acknowledge that persecution is to be expected by the Christian;
7. affirm the efforts of one another to confidently face the challenges to Christians in this world;
8. recognize the characteristics of humble service as demonstrated by their pastors;
9. discover the comfort and hope proclaimed in this epistle.

THE CROWNING GLORY (Objective 1)

Use this section to introduce the concept that Baptism, like the crowning of a homecoming queen, provides evidence of a prior election. Christians lack direct knowledge of their election by God, but they can certainly infer this on the basis of their baptism. Through faith bestowed on me in baptism, I can be confident that God has brought me to Himself because of His determination that, for the sake of the saving life and work of Christ, I should be His own and live under Him in His kingdom of grace.

A BRIEF REVIEW (Objective 2)

In this section, we review two previously discussed themes of election: (1) chosen to inherit salvation (sessions 19 and 20), and (2) chosen to be used as witnesses (session 20). The questions offer some guidance, but you will want to explore with students their own insights and thoughts.

1. Answers will vary widely. Avoid broad generalities and encourage specific examples of Christians living harmoniously in church, home, and school.

2. Again, answers will vary but seek to avoid pious platitudes.

3. Do spend considerable time in discussing this difficult advice to Christians. Few Christian living skills are stranger to our human nature than these.

4. Not only are we are blessed with the assurance of an eternal salvation, but we enjoy the presence and power of God's Spirit to help us meet the difficulties of life with confidence, joy, and victory.

5. We are to prepare for our opportunities to testify to our faith in Christ through regular study of God's Word, frequent use of the Sacrament of the Altar, and constant prayer.

6. Answers may vary, but the substance always is the Gospel of God's gracious love in Christ Jesus.

7. People are seldom, if ever, won for the Lord through religious arguments and debates. Remind students that they are called to be witnesses—not lawyers.

THE PLEDGE OF A GOOD CONSCIENCE (Objectives 3 and 4)

In this section Baptism is emphasized as the sign of eternal election. Refer often to the quotation from Luther's Small Catechism provided at the beginning of this session in the Student Book.

1. Christ died to pay in full our debt of sin in order to bring us to God.

2. Every person is born into this life as a blind, dead enemy of God with no possibility of coming to God on his own.

3. Jesus proclaimed His victory over all the powers of Satan and evil, including the conquest of sin, death, and hell.

4. The reference is to "He descended into hell."

5. The waters of the flood lifted the ark with Noah's family to safety.

6. The water of Baptism channels to us the fruits of Christ's redemptive work. All sins and evil lusts within us are conquered by the power of the Spirit and we are raised to a new life as new creatures—the children of God. Refer to the Catechism quotation.

7. With sin washed away by the Holy Spirit through the forgiving, saving waters of Baptism, the Christian now stands before God as a holy saint.

8. The resurrection of Christ assures us of God's acceptance of His sacrifice for the sin of all.

9. Jesus intercedes for us before the throne of God.

A CALL TO ARMS (Objectives 5, 6, and 7)

1. Christ humbly gave Himself up so that all people might be eternally saved from sin, death, and hell.

2. Through suffering Christians are often led to realize the relative unimportance of worldly matters,

and to place their priority on the things of God.

3. Students likely will note many striking similarities between the two apostles as they write of following the attitude of Christ.

4. Encourage students to provide specific examples from their lives. If there are no examples, could it be a sign that being a Christian makes no difference in their lives?

5. Most students will concede that it is very difficult to maintain a meaningful prayer relationship with God while engaged in sinful activity which separates us from Him.

6. The more one loves another person, the easier it is to forgive and to be understanding of that person's weaknesses.

7. Grumbling about the need to show hospitality robs this display of love of its integrity and joy.

8. Answers will vary, but encourage an open and frank evaluation of each student's abilities.

9. The ultimate purpose is "that in all things God may be praised through Jesus Christ" **(4:11).**

DON'T BE SURPRISED (Objective 6)

1. Jesus promises a reward in heaven.

2. Note the text. (Suffering as punishment for doing wrong is not a mark of discipleship.)

3. Judgment here may be seen as a time for evaluation. If trials in the Christian life are a test of faith, the results may be seen as a sort of "grading." Faithfulness in suffering, although not a meritorious work to earn salvation, is certainly an outward fruit that gives evidence of sincere faith.

4. Jesus described the Christian life as a narrow and difficult road which can only be successfully traveled by a few.

5. Answers will vary.

6. Answers will vary. Encourage much sharing.

7. Encourage students to mark these passages in their Bibles or to copy them in their notebooks. You might want to ask students to memorize several of them.

HUMBLE YOURSELVES AND BE LIFTED UP (Objectives 5, 8, and 9)

1. A pastor, like a shepherd, is to be a gentle leader and a humble persuader who leads by example and love.

2. Some of the characteristics which may be mentioned are self-sacrificing, courageous, caring, loving, and personal involvement.

3. Answers will vary. Students may mention the relatively low salary, the extra hours, the voluntary nature of many things he does, etc.

4. The pastor is to lead by example; he neither drives the flock from behind, nor gets out so far in front that he cannot be followed clearly.

5. They will be lifted up. Encourage students to tell what they think this means.

6. Relate this discussion to home, school, work, community, etc.

7. Ask students to identify some of their anxieties, and discuss how God's care for them might make it easier to cope with these fears.

8. Peter here refers to the confident faith. God's Word is the sword of the Spirit, and faith is a shield for the Christian (Cf. **Eph. 6:10–18**).

9. Emphasize the importance of the support system which we have in the church. We all can defeat Satan because of our common faith.

10. We have God's assurance that He will use the troubles of life to strengthen our faith.

CHAPTER 4
2 PETER AND JUDE

22. Twin Letters

CENTRAL TRUTH

In order to persevere against the subversive activity of false teachers in the church, Christians are to fortify themselves with a personal "knowledge" of Christ, based securely upon the foundation of God's inspired Word.

OBJECTIVES

That the students by the power of the Spirit will

1. discover the astonishing similarity between **2 Peter** and **Jude**;
2. summarize what is known of the historical setting of these two epistles;
3. recognize that to know Jesus is to trust in Him as Savior;
4. distinguish between natural and revealed knowledge of God;
5. affirm their confidence in the inspired Scriptures as the only reliable norm for true knowledge of God.

INTRODUCTION (Objective 1)

Use the opening paragraph to introduce students to the two books under consideration. If you are fortunate enough to have twins in your class or in your school, use them in a sensitive manner as an example of individuals who have striking similarities and yet who maintain unique qualities. Explain that the two letters you are about to investigate are also much alike and yet are distinctive.

THE HISTORICAL SETTING (Objective 2)

Identify Jude with what the students remember about James. Most of what was said about James is also true of Jude, except that the latter apparently did not have the stature of his more famous brother. He is, of course, named Judas in the **Mark 6:3** passage.

Review the meaning of the designation "general" for these epistles, and have the students note that no particular group of Christians is addressed. The internal evidence in the letters makes dubious any conclusion about the background or geographical location. Peter's reference in **3:1** to a previous letter may refer to **1 Peter,** but there is also much scholarly opinion that a lost third letter may be meant. Certainly, the almost identical wording of parts of the two letters suggests that they were not written to the same recipients.

Conservative scholars are uncertain as to which letter, **2 Peter** or **Jude,** antedates the other. In *The Concordia Self-Study Bible*, a note suggests the possibility that "While many have insisted that **Jude** refers to **Peter,** it is more reasonable to assume that the longer letter **(Peter)** incorporated much of the shorter **(Jude).**"

However, because of the almost direct quote of **2 Peter 3:3** in **Jude 18,** Donald Guthrie in his *New Testament Introduction* (p. 926) concludes, "If Peter wrote **2 Peter** for a certain constituency and shares the contents of his letter with Jude, suggesting that the latter use the passages about the false teachers in a letter to be sent to his own constituency, where the trouble-makers were not only threatening but were actively operative, all the phenomena would be accounted for."

KNOWING JESUS (Objective 3)

Be sure to emphasize the subject of knowledge with your students. Note that this idea is used as the connecting link throughout the study of these two letters. If students miss this point, they will miss the unifying factor of this and the following lesson. Call attention to the many references to knowledge throughout **2 Peter.**

1. The context would favor the conclusion that Peter is speaking of spiritual needs at this point. However, there is certainly room for other opinions from the students.

2. To be called is to be invited by the Holy Spirit through the Gospel to believe in Jesus Christ as one's personal Savior. Remind students of Luther's explanation of the Third Article: " . . . the Holy Ghost has called me by the Gospel . . . "

3. Answers will vary, but this can become a very meaningful exercise.

4. A rather clear reference to the partial restoration of the image of God which was lost when sin entered our first parents. The full restoration will not be ours until we reach glory.

5. Corruption is caused by evil desires. Compare also **Mark 7:20–23.**

6. Answers will vary, but a very fruitful discussion may result.

7. Peter uses the words **"near-sighted and blind."**

8. He has forgotten that **"he has been cleansed from his past sins."**

9. An obvious reference to the virtues mentioned in **verses 5–7.**

10. Another rich source of discussion material.

THE REVEALED KNOWLEDGE OF GOD
(Objectives 4 and 5)

1. An important subject to discuss. Many Lutheran high school students are tired of religion classes.

2. Scholarly opinions differ on this question, but it might be interesting to explore student views.

3. The two epistles of Peter in the canon are results of his efforts to make a lasting contribution. There is good evidence that Peter also was the guiding source for Mark's gospel.

4. Among events mentioned might be the miraculous catch of fish, the stilling of the storm, the post-resurrection appearances, and the ascension.

5. Judas' replacement was to have been one who had been with Jesus throughout His ministry (including His resurrection) so that his testimony would be that of an eyewitness.

6. The reference is to the transfiguration. John and James were present along with Peter.

7. We have been privileged to see the fulfillment of their prophecies in the person and life of Jesus Christ.

8. As a **"lamp to my feet and a light for my path."**

9. Probably a reference to this world, but this could also mean the spiritual darkness of our sinful nature.

10. When Jesus returns in glory, or when we leave this world to be with Him in heaven.

11. As we study the Bible, we are to interpret passages according to other passages that deal with the same subject. We are not to read into Scripture our personal pet ideas and biases.

12. While there are many who claim to speak for God and even insist that He speaks privately to them, we recognize no inspiration to people today that is equivalent to the Spirit's guidance to the human writers of Scripture.

COMPARING THE TWINS (Objective 1)

Assign this section for students to complete prior to the next session. This activity is designed to prepare students for the next lesson.

Jude 4	2 Peter 2:1
Jude 6	2 Peter 2:4
Jude 7	2 Peter 2:6
Jude 8	2 Peter 2:10
Jude 9	2 Peter 2:11
Jude 10	2 Peter 2:12
Jude 11	2 Peter 2:15
Jude 12a	2 Peter 2:13
Jude 12b–13	2 Peter 2:17

23. The Know-Nothings

CENTRAL TRUTH

Christians must be on the alert to identify and boldly confront those who would introduce doctrines of human invention into the church. Vigilant Christians have the confidence that God is with them now, and that He will grant them the final victory when Jesus returns in glory.

OBJECTIVES

That the students by the power of the Spirit will

1. recognize the spiritual dangers presented by false teachers in the church;
2. realize that most false teachings enter the church by subterfuge;
3. identify many of the false teachings which endanger the church today;
4. describe effective techniques to deal with corrupting influences within the church;
5. rejoice in the knowledge that God will ultimately deliver His church from all evil in the final judgement;
6. eagerly anticipate the early return of Christ.

INTRODUCTION (Objectives 1 and 2)

Begin this session by going through the matching assignment from the previous session. The extraordinary similarities suggest that Jude relied heavily on **2 Peter** in composing his letter (or vice versa). Or it may be that both men from their individual points of view were writing about matters of common knowledge in the early church. Other suggestions have been advanced. Inspiration does not imply some kind of mechanical dictation. Many of the writers of the Bible did research, and they used available sources in writing. Luke, for example, in the introduction to his Gospel indicates that he interviewed eyewitnesses and did other research before writing his account of the life and ministry of Jesus.

The theme of knowledge is continued. Many scholars believe that the heretics condemned in these letters represent an early form of Gnosticism. This word comes from the Greek word *gnosis* (knowledge) because these people claimed to have a higher knowledge of spiritual matters. It seems reasonable to conclude that Peter used the knowledge theme to point out that these men really lacked the essential knowledge of Christ. This suggests our theme of "know-nothings." The major errors of Gnosticism will be discussed later, but the teacher may introduce the term in connection with this discussion of knowledge.

EXAMINING THE FRUIT

Emphasize the fact that the most dangerous heresies enter the church secretly. Seldom do heretics at the outset openly attack the orthodoxy of the church. The following is a list of the teachings and practices to which these two letters allude:

1. refusal to submit to church authority **(Jude 8, 2 Peter 2:10)**;

2. licentiousness or freedom from obedience to God's law **(Jude 16, 2 Peter 2:18–19)**;

3. the claim to special visions **(Jude 8, 19; 2 Peter 2:3)**;

4. denial of the divinity of Christ **(Jude 4, 2 Peter 2:1)**;

5. freedom from the rule of "celestial beings" **(Jude 8, 2 Peter 2:10)**.

RECOGNIZING THE FRUIT
(Objectives 3 and 4)

1. A thorough knowledge of God's Word is the best defense against false teaching. Scripture is the Christians' norm by which they may **"test the spirits to see whether they are from God" (1 John 4:1)**.

2. Cults, such as Mormonism, New Age, and "Armstrongism," attract many followers. The names of contemporary movements change, but students will be able to name many current heresies.

3. Most are very bold in asking for financial contributions. The leaders often live in luxurious homes, travel first-class, and enjoy other trappings of wealth.

4. Many heretical leaders claim to receive special revelations from God in their prayer rooms. Some claim to be in contact with the spirits of the dead (New Age). Others, such as the Mormons, may claim such revelations as special visits from angels. Some may claim the ability to interpret tongues which are unintelligible to others.

5. Many heretical leaders avoid working in a denomination that provides doctrinal supervision.

6. Satanism is one extreme where evil is glorified. At the other end of the spectrum are those who ridicule the whole idea of a personal devil.

7. It should be obvious to students that many of the Eastern religions, as well as others that will be mentioned, are attracting young people at an alarming rate.

8. Freedom from the constraints of the Law.

9. Scripture makes it very clear that God will judge very harshly those who have enjoyed a personal relationship with Jesus and then rejected Him. On the other hand, God has also promised to support us in time of temptation and to provide the necessary spiritual strength to withstand the devil and his evil forces.

KNOWING THE ENDING (Objectives 5 and 6)

1. The Word of God created the world and will destroy it.

2. They see the world continuing as it has for generations; they see no evidence of Christ's return. Therefore, they are confident that this world age will continue as it has in the past.

3. In order to give more of His children an opportunity to come to faith (repentance).

4. Bringing the Gospel to more people will hasten Christ's return. The judgment will take place when the last of God's elect come to faith. (Read **2 Peter 3:12** within the context of **verses 8** and **9**.)

5. Some students may frankly express a lack of enthusiasm for the judgment. Be open and allow for a candid exchange of opinions and feelings.

6. Some Bible students who tend to believe that **2 Peter** was written before **Jude** appeal to this passage as possibly being a direct quote from **2 Peter 3:3**. Of course, this is speculative.

7. Christians are built up by regular and frequent use of Word and Sacrament.

8. What a great opportunity to elicit sharing of the Gospel between students. We are justified. Therefore we stand faultless, pure, spotless, and blameless before God by faith in the atoning and substitutionary sacrifice of Jesus.

9. This question is for open discussion. You might encourage students to write privately some resolutions for themselves.

ASSIGNMENT

Encourage students to read **1 John** prior to the next session.

CHAPTER 5
THE THREE GENERAL EPISTLES OF JOHN

24. The Love Letters of John

CENTRAL TRUTH

The apostle John urges Christians to rejoice in God's gracious love which led Him to send His Son to atone for our sin, and to respond to His sacrificial love through their lives of love to God and others. This response will lead true believers to shun the works of darkness, to freely confess our sins, to trust in the life and work of Christ for salvation and life, and to walk in the light with Jesus as the model.

OBJECTIVES

That by the power of the Spirit the students will

1. summarize the events in the life of John that show his maturation in the faith;
2. discover the similarities in thought between the Gospel according to St. John and the first epistle of John;
3. explain the meaning of the imagery of darkness and light as used by John in his first epistle;
4. describe the characteristic behaviors of walking in the light;
5. compare God's justice under the Law with His justice in the Gospel;
6. confess their sins and rejoice in God's forgiveness;
7. indicate a sincere determination with God's help to walk in the light.

INTRODUCTION (Objective 1)

The goal of this section is to introduce the students to the apostle John, and to show his gradual development into the great man of love who wrote these epistles. As you read through this material with the class, add any of your own insights into the character of John. Students are to look up the Scripture references and to review the events described. This activity need not require much time because students probably are already familiar with these events.

As you discuss the reference to **Luke 9:51–55**, point out that this was a Samaritan village and that the Samaritans were hated by the Jews. Could John have been prompted by some degree of religious or national bigotry, that he would desire to call down God's wrath on this village?

THE FIRST LETTER

Do not spend too much time in convincing the class that John is the author of this epistle. Later comparisons with the Gospel of John will leave no doubt as to the common authorship of these two books.

Remind students of the very harsh condemnation of early Gnosticism in **2 Peter** and **Jude**. Point out that John very probably deals with a similar heresy in this epistle. Ask them to take special note of the more gentle approach used by John as compared to the harsher tone of **2 Peter** and **Jude.**

As in previous sessions, the discussion questions may be used in any number of ways. In fact, if these sessions are to be completed in one class period it likely will be necessary to assign some of the questions for work outside of class. Do not feel too tightly bound to these questions. You or members of your class may want to make other significant points as the Holy Spirit leads you.

1. The author makes it clear that he was an eyewitness to the events in Jesus' ministry on earth.

2. The reference to **John 1:1–2** indicates that "the Word" is one of John's favorite expressions for Christ. Remind students of the argument in **Hebrews** that Jesus is the perfect messenger of God's Word to people.

3. "Life" is another of John's favorite expressions for Christ. Note that John did not invent this title; he only records for us Christ's own use of this word to define Himself and His mission.

4. We become one of the living stones in fellowship with other Christians through saving faith in the redemptive life and work of Christ created in us by the Holy Spirit through the Gospel.

5. John's joy would be complete if everyone who read his letter would by the Spirit be brought to, and sustained in, faith in Jesus Christ as their Savior, and would live a life worthy of their calling.

WALKING IN THE LIGHT
(Objectives 2, 3, 4, 5, 6, and 7)

Perhaps some students have listened to a scanner radio and will probably report the same experience. Discuss the reasons for the increase of criminal activity after dark. Ask for other examples where darkness is associated with evil. An interesting question to ask in a lighthearted way might be: "Why do students want the lights turned down very low at school dances?"

In order to establish the close relationship between this epistle and the Gospel according to St. John, spend some time with the verses from the Gospel.

1. John says that He received these words from Christ Himself.

2. Those who walk in the darkness engage in sinful activity forbidden by God.

3. There should be some discussion here of excommunication. This practice is designed to lead those who live in flagrant sin that reflects unbelief in the Savior to repent of their sin, return to the Savior, and seek to lead a more God-pleasing life. The purpose is not to embarrass, antagonize, or punish the wayward sinner. The motive is to be that of sincere love and concern for the eternal well-being of that person.

You may wish to review Jesus' teaching about this in **Matt. 18:15–17.**

4. Essentially, God's justice is His fairness in dealing with His creatures. When God deals with us in justice, He demands that we perfectly obey all His commands and fully follow His will. If we fail to do so, we bring upon ourself the result of such disobedience—alienation from God, the fruits of sin, divine condemnation and punishment, and, ultimately, eternal death.

The Gospel directs us to God's dealing with us in grace and mercy. To fulfill His justice, God gave up His Son Jesus Christ. In our place the God-man Jesus perfectly fulfilled all of the demands of God's law and will. As our substitute, Jesus suffered the just punishment for our sin through His vicarious suffering and death. He rose to proclaim to us all that through His substitutionary life, suffering, death, and resurrection, He fully, completely, and perfectly fulfilled all of the demands of the Father's justice in our behalf. Because He is just, God is also true to the promises He extends to us through the Gospel.

5. Many passages may be cited. Encourage use of the concordance to find several (e.g., **Ps. 14:1; 51:5; Eccl. 7:20**).

6. As sinful persons, we of ourselves can only plead guilty and ask for divine mercy. Jesus, the One who fulfilled all righteousness in our behalf and who endured the just punishment for our sin, effectively pleads for us before the Father.

7. Jesus' death atoned for the sins of all people. The only sin that condemns a person eternally is rejection of God's gracious offer of forgiveness and life for the sake of Jesus. The efficacy of the atoning work of Christ is not limited only to the elect, as taught by classic Calvinism.

8. Those who stubbornly reject God's offer of life and salvation for the sake of the merits of Christ thereby bring upon themselves death and eternal condemnation; they will not share in the benefits. One comparison is that of a person who is the beneficiary of a fortune, but fails to receive his inheritance because he cannot believe his good fortune and therefore fails to act on it.

9. God's love is made complete when the Spirit brings a person to saving faith in Jesus, and enables that individual to produce the fruits of righteousness in a Christian life.

10. Answers will vary.

11. Jesus' new command was: "Love one another."

12. Anger as well as destructive actions are sins against the Fifth Commandment.

Lustful thoughts as well as deeds violate the Sixth Commandment.

Any divorce, except in the case of unfaithfulness, is judged as causing adultery.

All oaths are forbidden, except those required to obey governmental authorities in keeping the Fourth Commandment.

We are to repay evil with good.

We are to love our enemies.

13. One who hates his brother. Even experts of emotional behavior emphasize the harm that destructive emotions, such as anger, hatred, and worry, can bring to to the person who keeps such feelings.

14. The basis for his confidence in his readers is their relationship with Jesus the Savior. He describes this relationship with such phrases as: **"your sins have been forgiven on account of His name," "you have known Him," "you have overcome the evil one," "you have known the Father," "you have known Him who is from the beginning," "you are strong," and "the Word of God lives in you."**

15. To know Jesus is to believe in Him as your personal Savior from sin.

16. It is foolish to love the world because it is so very uncertain and temporary.

25. Children of the Heavenly Father

CENTRAL TRUTH

Through saving faith in Jesus Christ bestowed upon by the Holy Spirit through the Word, we Christians live in an intimate family relationship with the heavenly Father and with our brothers and sisters in the faith. As children of God, we seek to model our lives after that of our Father.

OBJECTIVES

That the students by the power of the Spirit will

1. recognize the amazing grace that God has shown them by adopting them into His family;
2. acknowledge that this family relationship involves the responsibility of displaying the Christian family trait of unselfish love;

3. express confidence in their status as baptized children of God conferred by the Spirit through the Word;
4. identify antichristian forces active in the world today;
5. indicate an understanding of the enlightening work of the Holy Spirit;
6. describe ways in which they can demonstrate love for others;
7. acknowledge the Christian responsibility to test, on the basis of God's Word, the teachings that they hear and read.

INTRODUCTION (Objectives 1 and 2)

On basis of the introductory paragraphs initiate a discussion of the significance of a personal family relationship with God. A distinctive characteristic of Lutheran theology has always been its emphasis on the Father/child relationship with God, as opposed to the Ruler/servant relationship stressed in some theologies. Emphasize that God has chosen to relate to us as beloved children through no merit of our own, but solely by His grace.

ENEMIES OF GOD'S FAMILY
(Objectives 3, 4, and 5)

It will be important to tie this section in with the family theme by emphasizing the anointing mentioned in **1 John 2:20, 27**. The anointing refers to the enlightening activity of the Spirit through the Word. It includes the written or spoken Word, and the Word in Baptism and the Lord's Supper.

An interesting thought that cannot be proven is that this may include a baptismal reference related directly to the manner in which Christians were welcomed into the family of God. In his *Apostolic Tradition*, the Roman Christian Hippolytus described the baptismal liturgy used in second century Rome.

In this service it was customary to include an anointing with the oil of exorcism before the actual act of Baptism, and an anointing with the oil of thanksgiving following. It is possible to suggest that this practice of anointing may have been in effect at the time of John. If so, John's reference to Baptism may have been a reminder to his readers of their adoption into God's family at their baptism.

1. The New Testament consistently views the entire time between Christ's First and Second Comings as the end times.

2. It is vital for Christians always to expect the imminent return of Jesus. There is nothing that Satan would like better than for Christians to stop watching and praying for their Lord's speedy return.

3. Answers will vary, but many of the heresies discussed in connection with **2 Peter** and **Jude** may be mentioned.

4. Jesus made it clear that He is one with the Father, and that those who have seen Him have seen the Father **(John 14:8–10)**.

5. As mentioned earlier, this is an opportunity to direct the discussion toward Baptism, the act through which most believers enter the family of God.

6. The Gospel is the Good News of salvation through the atoning life and work of Christ through which the Spirit works, sustaining believers in the family of God.

7. Jesus promised the Holy Spirit. It is He who enlightens us with His gifts, allowing spiritually blind people to understand the Gospel. Without His enlightening activity, the Gospel would remain foolishness to us **(1 Cor. 1:18–25)**.

FAMILY TRAITS (Objectives 2 and 6)

Ask students to share examples of ways in which children resemble their parents. These may include physical characteristics as well as personality traits. Move from this discussion to the point that, as children of God, we should exhibit the personal traits of our heavenly Father.

1. Because they had been unfaithful to God, Adam and Eve were filled with fear and shame when God approached them after their fall into sin.

2. The "image of God" is the first description of this likeness to God.

3. Remind students that the original image of God was lost when our first parents fell into sin, but that it is restored in Christians through the sanctifying activity of the Holy Spirit. God declares us whole in justification, yet, as sinners, we mature toward God's holiness throughout our Christian life. When we do sin, we have forgiveness through Christ.

4. The life of the child of God is to be characterized by Spirit-motivated righteousness and love toward others. Unbelievers may also demonstrate outward goodness and love, but not in response to God's saving love and activity in Christ.

(For a more complete discussion of civil righteousness, see the Apology of the Augsburg Confession, specifically II 12; IV 21, 181, 238; XVIII 4.)

5. Answers will vary. Encourage positive sharing of happy family experiences.

6. Answers will vary. Urge specific examples and avoid pious generalities.

7. Same as number 6. Be sure to mention Lutheran World Relief and other agencies.

8. **"Therefore, there is now no condemnation for those who are in Christ Jesus" (Rom. 8:1).** By His saving life and work, Jesus frees us from the guilt and penalty of sin.

9. According to **1 John 3:23**, we are to live in faith (the right relationship with God) and in love toward one another (the right relationship with others).

10. The Holy Spirit motivates and empowers us by the Gospel to live a life of good works. (Sanctification in the narrow sense.)

RECOGNIZING FAMILY MEMBERS
(Objective 7)

As children of God, it is important for us to know our brothers and sisters. This is complicated by agents of Satan appearing in the church, posing as spokespeople for God. Constantly alert to this danger, we are to be discerning people who compare all teachings we hear to God's revelation in the Scriptures.

1. Paul warns us to expect the appearance of false prophets and demonic spirits, who serve Satan and seek to destroy the family of God.

2. The Gnostics who denied the true human nature of Christ and distorted the entire Gospel of salvation.

3. The Scriptures are to be the only rule and norm of Christian teaching.

4. The expression "from God" points, among other things, to the Father/child relationship we enjoy in Jesus by the work of the Holy Spirit.

5. The Gospel of Jesus Christ is always foolish to natural man. False teachings are popular with the world because they are based on human reason, or in other ways they pander to the self-centered instincts of people.

26. Smile! God Loves You!

CENTRAL TRUTH

God's unconditional love for sinners, which led Him to offer His Son as the atoning sacrifice for sin, motivates the Christian to love Him in return, to respond with genuine love for others, and to face the challenges of life with realistic confidence.

OBJECTIVES

That the students by the power of the Spirit will

1. identify the new command which Jesus gave His followers;
2. express gratitude for God's unconditional love for them;
3. summarize ways in which they can show genuine love for others;
4. celebrate the joy that comes from serving others;
5. express confidence in the sure truth of the Gospel;
6. pray for themselves and for others.

INTRODUCTION (Objectives 1 and 2)

Use the introduction to set the theme and tone for this session. The session is to be one of joyful celebration of God's boundless love for sinners—a love that led Him to give His most precious possession to ransom all people from the bonds of sins. Jesus' new commandment should be seen not as a burdensome demand, but as an opportunity to express gratitude for the unspeakable gift of His beloved Son.

In connection with the chopstick story, ask students to suggest ways in which they can feed each other.

GOD LOVES ME AND I LOVE THEE
(Objectives 1, 2, and 3)

Read through this section with the class and encourage discussion of whatever insights you and your students may have.

1. God is the ultimate source of all true love. Only those who have been born again by the faith-working activity of the Holy Spirit, who have come to know Jesus by the enlightening of the Spirit, can experience the joy of genuine love.

2. The subject of knowing God has been covered in earlier lessons, and includes the concept of faith in the atoning work of Christ. Faith without works is a dead faith; a lack of love toward others is an indication of a lack of faith in Christ.

3. God demonstrated His love for us by sending **"His one and only Son" (1 John 4:9)**.

4. There is an amazing correspondence between **1 John 4:9** and the "Gospel in a nutshell," **John 3:16**.

5. Answers will vary. Parents will probably be the most frequent examples, but try to elicit others.

6. Take the time to review this familiar passage in which the Lord makes it clear that we see Him whenever we find fellow human beings in need of our love and care. If we possess saving faith, we will serve fellow human beings because they are creatures of God.

7. Use this question to review the work of the Holy Spirit in enlightenment (knowing) and regeneration (new life). It is He who makes the foolishness of the Gospel comprehensible to people and works that faith which leads to rebirth.

8. Answers will vary, but certainly you will want to emphasize again the uselessness of human effort in conversion. Remind students that human love is often fickle and unreliable, whereas God's love is sure and steady. Even if the whole world should turn against us, we can always rely on our heavenly Father's love.

9. We all desperately need the love and support of other people, both of which are to be reflected within the fellowship of the communion of saints.

10. Answers will vary.

11. Our confidence will be based on the atoning death of Jesus. As forgiven people of God, we Christians know that **"there is now no condemnation for those who are in Christ Jesus" (Rom. 8:1)**.

12. The fear referred to here is the dread of punishment and God's wrath.

13. Christ suffered the punishment for sin once and for all on the cross, for the sake of which the Father has declared us justified (holy and not guilty).

14. God's love for us in Jesus Christ motivates us to love others.

15. Love is the summary of the commandments.

HE AIN'T HEAVY—HE'S MY BROTHER (Objectives 3 and 4)

Encourage students to share personal experiences. Examples may be as simple as washing the car for Dad in response to his generosity, or as profound as offering a kidney for a sibling who needs a transplant. Be sure to emphasize in this discussion the joy of serving Christ in response to His love for us.

ON THE WITNESS STAND (Objective 5)

There are some very difficult passages in this section; because of time restrictions, do not go into any lengthy details. Try not to get bogged down in a discussion of the textual difficulties in **verses 7–8**. Avoid the issue unless some students have the King James Version of the Bible; in which case it may be necessary to briefly explain that the reference to **"the Father, the Word, and the Holy Spirit"** is probably an editorial addition to the original text. The questions provided are designed to concentrate the study on a few significant ideas.

1. Most commentators identify water and blood with Christ's baptism and His death on the cross. The Gnostic heretics of John's day taught that the ordinary man Jesus was anointed as the Christ at His baptism and that God left Him before His death so that He died as an ordinary man. John wants to make it clear that Jesus was the Christ during His entire life on earth and still continues as such at the right hand of the Father.

2. Students should recall that the Holy Spirit appeared as a dove at Jesus' baptism.

3. In the early church, the Holy Spirit testified to the Gospel's truth by converting sinners to the faith of salvation by Jesus Christ. The testimony of the Spirit created faith.

4. The Holy Spirit still verifies the Gospel today by working faith in the heart and by giving Christians the ability to lead sanctified lives of good works. Seemingly miraculous conversions continue to take place which can only be explained in terms of the work of the Holy Spirit.

5. If Christ had not died to pay for our sins, we would still be lost and condemned. His baptism would have been of little use if He had not finished the work His Father sent Him to do.

6. At both events, the Father proclaimed, **"This is My Son, Whom I love; with Him I am well pleased."**

7. The most convincing testimony is the faith that each of us has in Jesus. Only the miraculous working of the Holy Spirit can give us the confidence that we feel in our hearts.

CONFIDENT PRAYER (Objective 6)

1. When we ask for such spiritual blessings as the forgiveness of sin or the strengthening of faith, we have God's assurance that these prayers are according to His will. However, when we ask for earthly blessings we must leave the final decision up to God, who knows what's best for us, and to submit ourselves to His will.

2. The present tense in **verse 15** and in the **Isaiah** passage both offer the comforting thought that our prayers, according to God's will, have already been answered even before we have asked.

3. Briefly review the sin against the Holy Spirit as discussed earlier in session 5.

4. Answers will vary. Be sure that spiritual as well as material needs of others are mentioned.

5. The beginning and ending thought of the epistle is that Christ is "eternal life."

6. Answers will vary.

27. The Second and Third Letters

CENTRAL TRUTH

Every Christian is to support the mission of the church as we together seek to bring the Gospel to all people. Each of us is to support enthusiastically all ministries to spread the Gospel. Also, we are to be alert that we do not inadvertently aid the cause of the enemies of Christ.

OBJECTIVES

That by the grace of God the students will

1. compare and contrast the themes of **2 John** and **3 John**;
2. recognize the need for enthusiastic support of legitimate ministries;
3. seriously consider the possibility of church work as a career;
4. summarize the settings of the last two epistles of John;
5. recognize the need for caution in deciding which ministries to support;
6. participate in the ministries of the church by prayer and financial support.

INTRODUCTION (Objectives 1, 2, and 3)

Use this section to introduce the themes of the last two letters of John. This is also an opportunity to lead students to seriously consider the possibility of serving God and His people in some ministry of the church.

THE SETTING OF THE LETTERS

1. The chosen lady and her children may refer to an individual Christian woman and her family, but

more likely this letter is addressed to a congregation and its members. The church is often spoken of as a woman in the New Testament, and the Roman persecutions may have made it necessary to conceal the identity of the specific congregation.

2. **3 John** is definitely addressed to a Christian gentleman named Gaius. He clearly was a dear friend of John and probably a leader in one of the congregations of Asia Minor.

3. The word used repeatedly is "truth." Remind students of the importance of the same word in John's first letter.

4. Students will probably mention some of the following phrases: **"whom I love in the truth,"** friends who **"send their greetings," "the elder," "walking in the truth," "I have much to write ... talk face to face,"** etc.

CAUTION: DECEPTION, DEAD AHEAD!
(Objective 5)

1. John mentions the denial of the true humanity of Christ, one of the major doctrinal heresies of the early Gnostics.

2. The Christian, by the power and help of the Holy Spirit, constantly works at living out his faith in Christ.

3. Those who go back are inclined to give up the realities of God's work in Christ (the Gospel); those who run ahead are those who lead people to depend upon their own works for salvation rather than those of Jesus the Savior. Both errors address the same sinful rejection of the Gospel.

4. Christians today may share in the wicked work of false prophets by working for, or contributing financial support to, those who deny the truths of the Gospel.

5. Many may be identified, of which a few are as follows: some of the cults which actively solicit donations in public places, highly questionable TV and radio ministries, organizations which provide abortions, and fund-raising on behalf of projects for liberation theology.

6. Information might be obtained from informed pastors, the organization's annual report that gives receipts and disbursements, material compiled by local government agencies that may include reports of complaints, and various other sources.

7. Because of fraudulent organizations, two problems occur. The true Gospel is confused with false doctrines, and people may distrust every ministry which needs help.

NOW, FULL SPEED AHEAD
(Objectives 2 and 6)

1. Ministers of the church are not to receive so much that they become rich and may thus establish an easy mode of life. Nor are they to be so poor that they become mean in spirit and lack the means to fulfill their responsibility to themselves, their family, church, and their community (cf. **1 Tim. 6:9–10**).

2. The Name refers to Jesus and His cause.

3. The pagans provided no help for spreading the Gospel.

4. Some adjectives that might be suggested are self-centered, ambitious, snobbish, malicious, bigoted, domineering, and power-mad.

5. Demetrius was probably an evangelist; possibly he carried this letter and sought hospitality from Gaius.

6. Answers will vary. Encourage such suggestions as: the welfare committee, evangelism teams, and prayer chains.

7. Discuss ways in which local congregations send a portion of their offerings to their Districts, use a portion of that money to fund ministries within their boundaries and another part to support the worldwide mission and ministry of the Synod. You might also discuss the growing needs of the church, and the decreasing support being given by congregations to efforts beyond their local parishes.

8. Such agencies include Lutheran World Relief, the Bethesda Lutheran Home, the Lutheran Layman's League, the Lutheran Women's Missionary League, and the Lutheran Bible Translators. Be sure to give non-Lutheran students an opportunity to mention worthwhile ministries in their churches.

9. Answers here will vary; some may mention organizations such as the Salvation Army and other charitable community agencies. Some discussion of true and false doctrine may again be necessary.

10. We share the Gospel with the world by word and deed. Some may tell the Good News. We have many opportunities to do voluntary work. Another opportunity is to donate used clothing and other helpful items.

11. This answer is to be confidential. However, it would be interesting to arrive at some kind of class average; you can do so by an anonymous method of collecting the data.

28. The General Epistles: A Review

The review in the Student Book is directly related to the test questions on the General Epistles offered for your use in session 29. You may either ask students to answer the review questions, or to be prepared to raise questions about those items of which they are unsure.

IDENTIFICATIONS AND DEFINITIONS

General epistle: Usually a letter which is not specific in its address. Note that **2 John** and **3 John** are exceptions to the rule.

Wisdom: Not to be confused with intelligence or learning. In Scripture, wisdom means **"acquiring a disciplined and prudent life, doing what is right and just and fair"** (Prov. 1:3).

Royal Law: **"Love your neighbor as yourself."** (James 2:8)

Cornerstone: A description of Christ. The most perfect stone used in a building to establish the lines for the walls.

Living stones: A description of the place given to individual Christians in the building of the church. Believers play a vital and contributing role as instruments of the Spirit in the expansion and development of the church.

Submission: The willing cooperation of Christians with other people so that each person may fulfill the responsibilities which they have been given. Specific examples given in Scripture are the mutual relationships of spouses, employees and employers, citizens and government officials, and older and younger people.

Hope: The confident assurance of God's love, acceptance, forgiveness, protecting presence, and divine providence, not only for the present but especially for the future.

Royal priests: One Scriptural description of Christians given to emphasize the direct approach to God that believers enjoy because of the atoning, saving, reconciling life and work of Christ.

Revealed knowledge: The knowledge of God that the Holy Spirit reveals to us through the Word. Divine revelation centers in the Gospel which proclaims our salvation in Jesus Christ in spite of our sin and utter unworthiness.

Natural knowledge: The imperfect knowledge of God's Law which all people can learn through their observation of God's created universe and through the testimony of their conscience.

Obey the Gospel: In this context, obey means to believe in Christ, trusting Him as our Savior.

Son of Thunder: The nickname given by Jesus to John. This is perhaps an indication of a fiery disposition.

New command: **"Love one another"** (1 John 3:11).

Maundy: From the Latin word for *commandment* to denote the new commandment to serve one another given by Jesus on Thursday of Holy Week.

Knowledge: A word Peter uses to describe faith.

Election: Before the world was made, God chose all those who would be saved by means of the atoning work of Jesus Christ.

Image of God: The state of perfection in which Adam and Eve were created and which was lost when our first parents fell into sin. It is restored in Christians through the work of the Holy Spirit as God declares us holy; yet, still sinners, we receive the Spirit's help as we mature toward a more complete measure of Christian living.

Justice of God: God's fairness. Under the Law it means that all sin must be paid for in full. The message of the Gospel is that Christ through His vicarious life, suffering, death, and resurrection fully satisfied all of the demands of the Father's justice. God is also fair in the sense that He is true to His promises in the Gospel which He will perfectly fulfill for each believer.

Diotrephes: The head of a local church whom John condemned for his failure to receive hospitably the evangelists who came into his territory and also failing to support them.

Gaius: The faithful Christian to whom John addressed his Third Epistle, and whom he commended for his support of traveling evangelists.

Demetrius: An evangelist (missionary) who likely was the bearer of John's letter to Gaius.

Silas: Assistant to Peter who likely assisted him in the writing of his first epistle.

James: Brother of Jesus and also of Jude. Rejected Jesus early in life, but was reported as being among the disciples after the resurrection. Became the leader of the church in Jerusalem.

Peter: An apostle noted for his spiritual lows and highs.

John: The apostle who outlived all the others and was known for his great kindness and love. Early in his life, however, he displayed a selfish and intolerant attitude toward others.

Jude: Another brother of Jesus. He wrote the epistle that bears his name.

QUESTIONS FOR REVIEW, REFLECTION, AND DISCUSSION

1. Review in the Student Book the introductory sections for each of the Biblical books being studied. You may wish to provide additional material from reference books.

2. **James:** "Reflecting Christian faith in action."

1 Peter: "Encouraging words of hope to Christians enduring persecution."

2 Peter: "The true knowledge of Christ as opposed to the false 'knowledge' of the early Gnostics."

1 John: "God loves us with a love that motivates us to love one another."

2 John: "Don't support false ministries."

3 John: "Generously support faithful ministers."

Jude: "A stern condemnation of false teachers."

3. Gratitude to God for His undeserved love motivates the Christian.

4. See the introductory material of each book in the Student Book. Again, you may wish to share additional material from reference books.

5. Answers will vary, but try to identify one or two distinctive characteristics of each book.

6. Government (a) may forbid what God allows, (b) may allow what God forbids, (c) may not command what God forbids, (d) may not forbid what God commands.

7. Baptism is my assurance that I am a child of God. Through Baptism the Holy Spirit worked faith in my heart. Through this sacrament I received forgiveness of sin, acceptance into the family of God, motivation for a godly life, and the new life that culminates in heaven. Luther's Small Catechism offers a beautiful exposition of the significance of Baptism for the Christian life. You may wish to expand on that.

8. As strangers in the world we can expect persecution. As God's children we can also expect God's loving discipline. Although we certainly are not to seek suffering, yet, if God permits trials to befall us, we can be confident that God has our best interests as His concern.

9. Christ descended into hell to proclaim victory over Satan and all evil. You may wish to review the treatment of this doctrine in the Formula of Concord.

10. **2 Peter 2** and **Jude** are very similar. This suggests that one used the other as a source; probably **Jude** used **2 Peter.**

11. Adoption into God's family is an undeserved honor which brings unbounded joy to the Christian. It also brings an obligation to live in such a way that God's name will be honored and not shamed.

12. Christians are to be discerning and not swallow hook, line, and sinker the statements of every religious cause that they hear or read. Rather, they are to carefully test the spirits to be certain that they are proclaiming God's Word in its truth and purity. When one is convinced that this is the case, generous support is a privilege.

13. "Love" summarizes all of the commandments.

14. We all fail miserably to live up to the high standards of God's law.

15. The Christian sees the keeping of God's law not as an unescapable burden, but as a glorious opportunity to express gratitude to God.

16. All favoritism is forbidden by God.

17. As a stranger on earth, a Christian holds beliefs, attitudes, values, moral standards, and other ways of thought and action that are radically different from unbelievers.

18. Peter uses the flood event as a figure of Baptism.

19. Most false teachings enter the church hidden under the guise of truth and sincerity.

20. Several characteristics might be mentioned. Heretical movements tend to appeal to the young, attract large followings, claim special revelations denied ordinary people, and promise special rewards to the true believers. Heretical movements differ from schismatic movements in that heretical movements tend to center on teachings, and schismatic movements tend to focus on one or more persons with extraordinary powers of persuasion.

21. Evil is often associated with darkness. The Christian walks in the light of the Gospel and God's entire Word to avoid all evil.

22. Jesus says that we see Him whenever we have the opportunity to assist any of our fellow human beings, all of whom God created. Be sure to note that this teaching of our Lord does not teach salvation by works. Rather, it teaches that a natural outcome of a right relationship with God through Jesus Christ is service to others.

23. God testified to Christ at His baptism, at His transfiguration, in the resurrection, in the outpouring of the Spirit at Pentecost, in the true faith that Christians have received from the Spirit, etc.

24. As Christians selecting a career in life, we are to reflect on the talents, abilities, skills, interests, and other attributes we possess. Then we are to consider how we can best use for God's purposes in the world the qualities which He has given us. We do well to give first consideration to a profession within the church, but, whatever vocation we choose, it is to be regarded as a calling wherein we will serve God.

29. Test: The General Epistles

Name _____ Hour _____

TRUE/FALSE

Decide whether each of the following statements is true or false. If it is true, put a plus sign (+) on the line provided. If it is false, put a zero (0).

___ 1. The writer of the epistle of James was an apostle.

___ 2. True faith in the heart will produce a life of good works.

___ 3. The recipients of the epistle of James were likely of Hebrew descent.

___ 4. The epistle of James was probably the first New Testament book to be written.

___ 5. The epistle of James bears a striking resemblance to Jesus' Sermon on the Mount.

___ 6. The writer of the epistle of James probably learned the teachings of Jesus by hearing most of the Lord's sermons.

___ 7. In the Bible, the word "wisdom" refers to intelligence.

___ 8. In the epistle of James, "royal law" means the Ten Commandments.

___ 9. Humility is a virtue to be highly desired by Christians.

___ 10. The first letter of Peter is addressed to the Christians of Rome.

___ 11. The first letter of Peter stresses the believer's confident hope.

___ 12. In writing his first epistle, Peter was assisted by Luke.

___ 13. Peter compares the church to a building in which the believers represent the cornerstone.

___ 14. Our earthly government may not forbid what God allows.

___ 15. The Bible teaches that Christian husbands and wives are to submit themselves to each other so that they can live together cooperatively and harmoniously.

___ 16. Christians become "royal priests" on the day of their confirmation.

___ 17. Suffering in the life of a Christian is a punishment for sin.

___ 18. Jesus descended into hell in order to proclaim victory over Satan.

___ 19. Jude was a brother of Jesus.

___ 20. The letter of Jude is nearly identical to parts of the letter of James.

___ 21. The Bible is the source of our "revealed knowledge" of God.

___ 22. In the Bible, the expression "obey the Gospel" means to live a life of good works.

___ 23. Both **2 Peter** and **Jude** contain stern condemnations of pagan people who are persecuting the Christians.

___ 24. John lived longer than any of the other apostles.

___ 25. When John was young, his fiery disposition earned him the nickname "Son of Thunder."

___ 26. John never refers to himself by name in the Bible.

___ 27. John emphasizes the family relationship we enjoy with our heavenly Father.

___ 28. In his first letter, John warns Christians not to show hospitality to false teachers.

___ 29. All teachings in the church should be judged according to the standard of God's Word, the Bible.

___ 30. The new command which Jesus gave His followers was about our salvation.

___ 31. The word "maundy" comes from a Latin word meaning "Thursday."

___ 32. The word "love" summarizes all of God's commandments.

___ 33. The second and third letters of John deal with the subject of the Christian's support of evangelism in the church.

___ 34. Those who are not called into the professional ministry still have a vital role to play in the mission of the church.

___ 35. John addressed his second letter to his good friend Diotrephes.

MULTIPLE CHOICE

Choose the BEST ending for each of the following statements and print the letter of your choice on the line provided.

___ 36. A general epistle is one which is
   A. usually addressed to a specific person.
   B. usually addressed to a specific congregation.
   C. usually not specific in its address.
   D. not written by an apostle.

___ 37. The central theme of the letter of James is
   A. "beware of false prophets."
   B. "hope springs eternal."
   C. "love your neighbor as yourself."
   D. "living your Christian faith."

___ 38. Christians should lead God-pleasing lives because
   A. otherwise they will not be forgiven.
   B. God threatens to punish sinners.
   C. it will improve their self-concept.
   D. they are grateful for God's gift of forgiveness.

___ 39. Measured against the standard of God's law, most of us

A. fail the test badly.
B. are not perfect, but do pretty well.
C. are excellent examples to others.
D. are forgiven by God's grace.

___ 40. For the Christian, keeping God's law
A. is a tiresome burden.
B. is quite easy.
C. is unnecessary.
D. is a joyful privilege.

___ 41. Favoritism in the Christian church is
A. an acceptable way to recognize generous offerings.
B. neither forbidden nor commanded in the Bible.
C. hardly ever encountered.
D. forbidden by the Lord.

___ 42. The Christian virtue of submission means
A. never expressing strong opinions.
B. being seen, but not heard.
C. placing as much importance on the interests of others as on your own.
D. avoid taking leadership responsibilities.

___ 43. In discussing the concept of wisdom, James
A. discourages seeking it.
B. speaks of earthly wisdom and heavenly wisdom.
C. says that it is found mainly in the uneducated.
D. none of the above.

___ 44. The fact that we are strangers in the world should cause Christians to
A. separate themselves from the world as much as possible.
B. expect some people to consider them peculiar.
C. hate every moment of their lives.
D. give up any hope of influencing others.

___ 45. The life of Peter can be described as
A. one of constant spiritual strength.
B. one of constant spiritual weakness.
C. a series of spiritual lows and highs.
D. lonely and depressing.

___ 46. From eternity God chose and elected
A. those who would be adopted as His children.
B. all people to be adopted as His children.
C. those who would not be saved.
D. both A and C.

___ 47. God chose and elected you because
A. He foresaw that you would respond favorably to the Gospel.
B. He knew that you would be baptized.
C. of His merciful gracious love.
D. He knew that you would be an obedient child.

___ 48. As living stones we Christians are
A. mainly ornaments to make the world a better place.
B. placed in the pathway of the ungodly so that they will stumble spiritually.
C. important, contributing members of the church.
D. a minor, unimportant part of the church.

___ 49. A Christian's baptism is like a crown which
A. shows the world that we are better than other people.
B. gives daily assurance that we are people of God.
C. gives us authority over other people.
D. is given to us by our parents.

___ 50. Peter used the Old Testament story of Noah and the flood as a figure of
A. Christ's death.
B. Christ's resurrection.
C. the final judgment.
D. Baptism.

___ 51. When the Bible speaks about knowing Jesus it means
A. the ability to relate the main events of His life.
B. having faith in Him as one's personal Savior.
C. being physically near Him during His life on earth.
D. none of the above.

___ 52. Human beings, by nature, have
A. absolutely no knowledge of God.
B. a partial knowledge of God, but only of His law.
C. a complete knowledge of God.
D. a partial knowledge of God's law and gospel.

___ 53. When Adam and Eve sinned they lost the image of God, which is now
A. partially restored in Christians.
B. partially restored in all people.
C. completely gone from all people.
D. none of the above.

___ 54. Most false teachings enter the church
A. disguised as the truth.
B. by openly attacking established doctrines.
C. through in-depth study of the Scriptures.
D. through laypersons who have not studied the Bible as thoroughly as pastors.

___ 55. Many false prophets
A. direct their efforts toward young people.
B. claim that they receive private revelations from God.
C. quickly attract large numbers of followers.
D. all of the above.

___ 56. The apostle John describes the Christian life as
A. a war between the forces of good and evil.
B. walking in the light.

     C. a race with heaven as the finish line.
     D. mountain climbing.
___ 57. God's justice under the Gospel requires Him to forgive us, because
     A. we have tried hard to obey Him.
     B. our sins have been fully paid for by Jesus.
     C. His law is so strict that no one can keep it perfectly.
     D. the Law has been abolished by Jesus.
___ 58. The most comforting thing about being invited to call God "Father" is that
     A. it reminds us of the warm and loving relationship we have with Him.
     B. it reminds us that God is the final authority who must be obeyed at all times.
     C. it emphasizes His masculinity and strength.
     D. we can be sure that He will always be as reliable as our earthly fathers.
___ 59. As God's adopted children, it is reasonable to assume that Christians will
     A. always be as perfect as He is.
     B. rebel against His authority.
     C. display His family traits.
     D. be jealous of their brothers and sisters in the faith.
___ 60. Jesus said that, in a way, we see Him whenever
     A. we encounter one of our fellow human beings in need of our help.
     B. we read religious books.
     C. we contribute money for the work of the church.
     D. we close our eyes in prayer.
___ 61. God testified to the truth of Jesus' claims about Himself
     A. in a voice heard at the Lord's baptism.
     B. in a voice heard at the Lord's transfiguration.
     C. by giving miraculous powers to the apostles at Pentecost.
     D. all of the above.
___ 62. Able Christians should generously support any ministry which
     A. claims to represent Jesus in the world.
     B. has the support of large numbers of people.
     C. they have carefully evaluated on the basis of the Word of God.
     D. uses the Bible in its public activities.
___ 63. The first consideration for Christian young people deciding on a life's career should be
     A. what career enables them best to serve God.
     B. what career provides the most financial rewards.
     C. what career will be in the most demand in the future.
     D. what career will be the most intellectually stimulating.

MATCHING

Use your knowledge of the general epistles to match each of the books listed below with the characteristic quotations which follow. Indicate your choice by printing the appropriate letter on the blank provided.

A. James   D. First John
B. First Peter   E. Second John
C. Second Peter F. Third John
                   G. Jude

___ 64. "Dear friend, you are faithful in what you are doing for the brothers, even though they are strangers to you. They have told the church about your love. You will do well to send them on their way in a manner worthy of God."
___ 65. "In His great mercy He has given us new birth into a living hope through the resurrection of Jesus Christ from the dead, and into an inheritance that can never perish, spoil or fade—kept in heaven for you."
___ 66. "What good is it, my brothers, if a man claims to have faith but has no deeds? Can such faith save him?"
___ 67. "In the very same way these dreamers pollute their own bodies, reject authority and slander celestial beings. But even the archangel Michael, when he was disputing with the devil about the body of Moses, did not dare to bring a slanderous accusation against him, but said, 'The Lord rebuke you!'"
___ 68. "If anyone comes to you and does not bring this teaching, do not take him into your house or welcome him. Anyone who welcomes him shares in his wicked work."
___ 69. "If we claim to have fellowship with Him yet walk in the darkness, we lie and do not live by the truth. But if we walk in the light, as He is in the light, we have fellowship with one another, and the blood of Jesus, His Son, purifies us from all sin."
___ 70. "For this very reason, make every effort to add to your faith goodness; and to goodness, knowledge; and to knowledge, self-control . . . For if you possess these qualities in increasing measure, they will keep you from being ineffective and unproductive in your knowledge of our Lord Jesus Christ."

Answer Key: Test on the General Epistles

TRUE/FALSE

1. 0	13. 0	25. +
2. +	14. 0	26. +
3. +	15. +	27. +
4. +	16. 0	28. 0
5. +	17. 0	29. +
6. 0	18. +	30. 0
7. 0	19. +	31. 0
8. 0	20. 0	32. +
9. +	21. +	33. +
10. 0	22. 0	34. +
11. +	23. 0	35. 0
12. 0	24. +	

MULTIPLE CHOICE

36. C	46. A	55. D
37. D	47. C	56. B
38. D	48. C	57. B
39. A	49. B	58. A
40. D	50. D	59. C
41. D	51. B	60. A
42. C	52. B	61. D
43. B	53. A	62. C
44. B	54. A	63. A
45. C		

MATCHING

64. F	67. G	69. D
65. B	68. E	70. C
66. A		

CHAPTER 6
THE REVELATION OF SAINT JOHN

30. The Mystery Book of the New Testament

CENTRAL TRUTH

By the inspiration of the Holy Spirit God has provided His people with John's book of **Revelation,** the comforting message of hope in the face of persecution.

OBJECTIVES

That the students by the power of the Spirit will
1. identify the human author of **Revelation** and the original recipients of this letter;
2. describe the circumstances of the original recipients that created a need for this letter;
3. identify at least two purposes the author sought to achieve through this letter; and
4. describe circumstances today similar to those of first century Christians that make this letter relevant for Christians of the 20th century.

BACKGROUND

For this section of the course you need ready access to sound Bible commentaries and other reference books. We suggest the following:

Becker, Siegbert W. *Revelation.* Milwaukee: Northwestern, 1985. (An excellent, popular, dependable commentary.)

Caird, G. B. *The Revelation of St. John the Divine.* San Francisco: Harper and Row, 1966. (A standard commentary conservative in interpretation but somewhat liberal in theology.)

Franzmann, Martin H. *The Revelation to John.* St. Louis: Concordia, 1976. (A brief, popular verse-by-verse commentary.)

Hendriksen, W. *More Than Conquerors: An Interpretation of the Book of Revelation.* Third Edition. Grand Rapids: Baker, 1944. (An excellent popular theological exposition of Revelation. Used extensively in the preparation of the study guide.)

Lenski, R. C. H. *The Interpretation of St. John's Revelation.* Columbus: Lutheran Book Concern, 1935. (Although one may not agree with all of the author's conclusions, this is a conservative, useful book.)

Mounce, Robert H. *The Book of Revelation.* The New International Commentary on the New Testament. Grand Rapids: William B. Eerdmans, 1977. (A conservative, useful commentary from the perspective of Reformed theology.)

Poellot, Luther. *Revelation: The Last Book in the Bible.* St. Louis: Concordia, 1962. (A popular study of Revelation originally offered to a Bible class in a congregational setting.)

Swete, Henry B. *The Apocalypse of St. John.* Third Edition. London: MacMillan, 1908. Reprinted by William B. Eerdmans, Grand Rapids, 1968. (One of the best technical commentaries. Used extensively in the preparation of this section.)

In addition, you may wish to consult books on New Testament introduction and Bible dictionaries for background material on the book.

**THE MYSTERY BOOK
OF THE NEW TESTAMENT**

After the students have read this section, ask them what comes to their minds when they think about the book of **Revelation.** Follow up by asking them what they hope to learn from this course.

WHO WROTE REVELATION? (Objective 1)

1. The Bible passages clearly identify the writer as John.

2. The material in the Student Book introduces the question of which John wrote this book. In this course we accept the traditional view that it was John the apostle, but the possibility of John Mark or John the Elder is noted. From Scripture we know the following about the apostle John:

a. John was the brother of the apostle James. They were the sons of Zebedee and had been engaged in the fishing business with their father. When Jesus called them, they left without delay to follow Him **(Mark 1:19–20.)**

b. John, together with James and Peter was an eyewitness to the transfiguration of Jesus **(Luke 9:28–29).**

c. There was a special bond between John and Jesus. He reclined next to Jesus at the Last Supper and was referred to as the **"disciple whom Jesus loved" (John 13:23).**

d. Because John was known to the high priest, he was able to follow Jesus into the high priest's courtyard on the night before His death **(John 18:15).**

e. Jesus gave the care of His mother over to John upon His death, and John took Mary into His home **(John 19:26–27).**

f. John outran Peter to the tomb on the first Easter morning **(John 20:1–10).**

g. John was the first to recognize the risen Lord when he appeared to the disciples on the Sea of Tiberias **(John 21:1–7).**

h. After Pentecost, John was with Peter at the healing of the man at the temple **(Acts 3:1–10).**

3. This paragraph provides a brief summary of John's later life. In view of the many frivolous views concerning "love" today, you may want to ask students to distinguish "love" as often understood now, and "love" as understood by John.

4. Have students look up the listed passages to note the supernatural, divine source of John's visions which he wrote **"in the Spirit" (1:10).**

FOR WHOM WAS REVELATION WRITTEN?
(Objectives 2–3)

Ask students to look up the Bible references to the seven churches in **Rev. 2:1, 8, 12, 18; 3:1, 7, 14.** Have them locate on a map the province of Asia and the seven cities addressed by John.

In addition to the material in the students' text, you may wish to draw from other books to describe the conditions of the world and of the church at the time John wrote **Revelation.**

You might also ask students to compare the conditions of Christians in the late first century with those of Christians in many parts of the world today.

THE PURPOSE OF THE LETTER
(Objective 3)

1. Briefly survey the cited passages and the persecutions of Christians throughout human history. Draw attention to the crass persecution of Christians in such traditional Christian nations as East Germany (the heart of Luther's Reformation) and Russia. But also focus on the many subtle ways that Christians are persecuted in Canada or the United States when they seek to reflect their faith in everyday life.

2. Emphasize that a major purpose of **Revelation** is to encourage Christians to remain steadfast in their faith in spite of opposition, ridicule, and persecution. A second purpose is to stimulate Christians to be energetic in fulfilling the missionary opportunities of the church in view of the horrendous future that awaits all who reject the Gospel of Christ, and to see the wonderful blissful future that lies ahead for all the people of God.

3. Conclude by having students look up the passages from **Revelation** listed here. Talk with them about the bliss of heaven which awaits us as believers in Jesus. Pray that through your study of **Revelation** the students will be led by the Spirit to value more fully their relationship with God through Christ, and to share the Gospel of Christ with those who do not know Him.

3:20–22—"Here I am! I stand at the door and knock." The Gospel call is for everyone as Jesus desires to make His home is each person's heart.

4:11—Revelation includes beautiful words of praise to God, of which this verse is an example.

5:9–10—Through His sacrificial death, Jesus has purchased for God people of every tribe and language and people and nation.

7:9–17—We gain a glimpse of the splendor of our life in heaven in the presence of almighty God where we will experience neither hunger, thirst, discomfort, nor tears.

21:1–4—We see the imagery of Christ the bridegroom coming to take His bride, the Church, to live with Him in eternal happiness.

22:1–6—Heaven is a glorious place. Here we will have no need of the light of lamp or sun, for the Lord God will give us light.

22:17—The gift of eternal life through the merits of Christ is free to all through faith in Christ Jesus.

ASSIGNMENT

These are suggested assignments for the students.

1. Quickly scan through the entire book of **Revelation** before the next class session.

2. With the help of a Bible dictionary and similar reference materials write a brief biography of the apostle John.

3. Locate on a map the province of Asia and the seven cities to which John wrote.

31. Clues for Solving the Mystery

CENTRAL TRUTH

Although evil and Satan run rampant in this present age, God is still in control; the exalted Christ is present among His people and rules all things for the ultimate welfare of His followers.

OBJECTIVES

That the students by the power of the Spirit will

1. describe the nature of apocalyptic literature;
2. demonstrate their understanding of the symbolic language and numerals used in **Revelation;**
3. define the four approaches often used in interpreting **Revelation;**
4. recognize the organizational structure of the book of **Revelation.**

CLUES FOR SOLVING THE MYSTERY

Point out that many people are intimidated by **Revelation,** or misunderstand it, because they lack understanding of its distinctive literary qualities and its use of symbolic language and numbers. Note that during this session students will be introduced to those explanations necessary to understand, interpret, and apply this book to their Christian faith and life.

TYPE OF LITERATURE (Objective 1)

You might draw attention to the descriptions of five general aspects of apocalyptic literature given in the text. Then ask students to look up one or more of the Bible passages that are listed at the beginning of this section to identify which aspects of apocalyptic literature are to be found in these individual passages. For example, **1 Thess. 4:13–17** is eschatological. It implies that our best hope lies in a future world rather than in this one (pessimism concerning humankind's ability to produce peace and righteousness in this age). It points to a divine plan moving according to a predetermined schedule and end, and is somewhat esoteric and symbolic in language (e.g., **"will be caught up . . . in the clouds to meet the Lord in the air" [v. 17]**).

Then, discuss with your class both the similarities and the differences between **Revelation** and apocalyptic literature in general.

THE LANGUAGE OF REVELATION (Objective 2)

Throughout your study of **Revelation,** you will encounter a variety of symbols unfamiliar to your students. In the appropriate places these symbols will be explained. But it will be desirable for your students at the outset to be prepared to meet with this symbolic language.

Use of such language is rather common today. For example, we speak of the Chicago Bears or the St. Louis Cardinals. Immediately we think of a football or baseball team—not animals. So in John's day people undoubtedly recognized immediately the figures of speech he used. You may think of other examples of symbolic language intelligible to your class which we use today.

FOR DISCUSSION

1. Examples of "Babylon" in our contemporary world are those governments that persecute Christians. Discuss student responses.

2. Though subtle, forms of persecution of the people of God exist even in a country which permits the free exercise of religion. Examples include the scheduling of sporting events on Sunday mornings, exposure to a media which mocks Christ and His followers, and peer pressure to break God's commandments.

3. God promises His power so that nothing will be able to separate us from His love in Christ Jesus, our Lord **(Rom. 8:35–39).**

THE USE OF NUMBERS (Objective 2)

A major pitfall in the study of **Revelation** lies in the interpretation of the numbers found within it. The Student Book describes some understandings of the symbolism of numbers in **Revelation.** At appropriate places throughout the course additional information will be given to help you interpret numbers as used by John in a responsible fashion.

APPROACHES TO THE INTERPRETATION OF REVELATION (Objective 3)

One's understanding of **Revelation** is guided by the person's approach to the book. The Student Book identifies and describes the four major approaches to **Revelation,** and indicates that each approach has its strengths and limitations. The approach used in the preparation of this section is a combination of the best of the four approaches.

The cyclical approach is important. Please give special attention to this aspect of the book. Each cycle begins with the ascension of Christ and ends with the Last Day. Carefully study the outline in the Student Book both to gain a grasp of the logical development of the book, and to note the several cycles.

Be sure that the students discuss these several approaches so that they will have opportunity to formulate a proper approach for themselves.

AN OVERVIEW (Objective 4)

Before the session carefully reflect on the outline given in the Student Book. As part of your preparation, scan the book of **Revelation** to see how this book fits in with the outline. If possible, it would be desirable to have students in class also scan the book to understand better how the outline fits the book.

Before the conclusion of the session, emphasize that the study of the book is not to be a mere academic exercise, but that as they read the book students and instructor are to ask at every point, "What does this mean? What does this mean for my personal life today?"

This outline was followed in the development of the study of **Revelation,** so you will want to refer to it frequently during the coming weeks.

ASSIGNMENT

1. Carefully read **Rev. 1:1–3:22** before the next session.

2. From a Bible dictionary or commentary learn what you can about the seven churches addressed by John in **Revelation 2–3.**

3. In an encyclopedia or history read about Domitian and other first century Roman emperors.

32. Preparing for the Truth

BIBLE BASIS
Rev. 1:1–3:22

CENTRAL TRUTH
Even as the divine Jesus reigned also while on the cross, so His people live and reign in and with Him even in the midst of suffering and death.

OBJECTIVES
That the students by the power of the Spirit will
1. identify three ways in which John prepared his readers for his message;
2. describe the authorship and purposes of the book of **Revelation,** and the circumstances under which this revelation was given;
3. explain the symbolic language of **Revelation 1**;
4. describe the structure of the specific letters to each of the churches;
5. discuss the specific circumstances and needs of each of the churches;
6. Identify the individual message given to each of the seven churches;
7. describe three personal spiritual lessons derived from the letters to the seven churches.

PREPARING FOR THE TRUTH
(Rev. 1:1–3:22, Objective 1)

Review with your class the content of the introductory paragraphs. Emphasize that before John shared the revelations given him, he first prepared his readers by establishing his authority and credentials, and cultivated the proper receptive attitude and disposition within the readers.

PROLOGUE (Objectives 2–3)
1. a. The ultimate source is God who, in His Son Jesus Christ, gave this revelation by His angel. The angel was commissioned by Jesus to guide John in his visions of heaven, of the earth, of the wilderness, and of the new heaven and new earth (see also **Rev. 1:10; 4:1; 10:4, 8; 11:1; 19:9; 22:8–9**).

b. The purpose was to show John and, through him, other believers "what must soon take place." Those who read and heed this prophecy will be blessed, especially when the days of crisis draw near.

c. Christians are encouraged to remain steadfast in spite of persecution (**2:10**), and to anticipate eagerly in faith the Second Coming of Jesus (**22:20**).

d. The angel revealed the visions to John who, in turn, bore witness to the Word of God and testimony of Jesus Christ which he received.

e. The Word of God and testimony of Jesus Christ.

f. For John's immediate hearers the crisis likely was the persecutions they soon would be called upon to endure. Ultimately, the crisis is the Second Coming of Jesus which will be preceded by great affliction. Every generation bears afflictions to remind them that the Second Coming is at hand. (In a sense, the Christian's death is a time of the Second Coming.)

g. The writer was John. Because of the authority John claimed for himself, and the acceptance his letter received, he probably was John the apostle.

2. Take time to explain to students the symbolism and meanings expressed in **1:4–8** as explained in the students guide.

JOHN'S CALL TO HIS PROPHETIC MISSION
(Objectives 2–3)

Present in your own way the material in this part of the students guide. Note the Old Testament parallels. Lead students in discussion of the three questions at the end of this section.

1. John fell as though dead at Jesus' feet, when He saw Jesus (**1:17**). Great respect and awe was shown by this action.

2. Jesus told John, **"Do not be afraid. I am the First and the Last. I am the Living One; I was dead, and behold I am alive for ever and ever! And I hold the keys of death and Hades (1:17b–18).**

3. Jesus told John to write what he had seen (**1:19–20**).

THE LETTERS (Objective 4)
Note the six common elements that appear in the seven letters. If you wish, ask students to read each of the letters with these elements in mind.

EPHESUS (Objectives 5–6)
This city was wealthy and magnificent; it was especially known for its shrine of Diana. Located near the west coast of Asia Minor, it not only was a major port, but it also was at the center of land routes to the most important cities of Asia Minor. Paul first visited this city about A.D. 52 during his second missionary journey, and spent about three years there during his third missionary journey. After his release from his first imprisonment in Rome, Paul likely had several brief visits, and left his close friend Timothy in charge of this church (**1 Tim. 1:3**). One of his best known letters is addressed to the Ephesians.

John went to Ephesus probably soon after the beginning of the Jewish revolt (A.D. 66). During the reign of Domitian (81–96) John was banished to Patmos where he received **Revelation.**

1. He "holds the seven stars in His right hand and walks among the seven golden lampstands." Christ rules the angels of these churches (the seven stars)

and is present in the midst of these churches (seven golden lampstands).

2. The Ephesian Christians labored, were patient in the midst of suffering, and were uncompromising over against evil. In their concern for truth, they tested those who claimed to be apostles, and hated the deeds of the Nicolaitans (likely heretics who taught what they thought people wanted to hear, possibly also for self-gain, and compromised with the sins of the world; they tried to serve both God and mammon).

3. In their zeal for truth the Ephesians seemed to have become loveless in their attitudes toward, and relationships with, one another and Christ.

4. If the Ephesians failed to repent, Jesus would remove the lampstand. A church may teach the Word faithfully, but in its "dead orthodoxy" and lack of love may "self-destruct."

5. Jesus promised them the Spirit who would give them victory over their lovelessness and the gift of eternal life.

6. Give students opportunity to apply this message to the church of today.

SMYRNA (Objectives 5–6)

Located on an arm of the Aegean Sea, Smyrna rivaled Ephesus as a commercial city. Located in a beautiful setting, it boasted of being the "First City of Asia in beauty and size." It sloped from the sea with its beautiful public buildings located on the rounded top of the hill Pagus. The westerly breeze kept it cool and comfortable throughout the year. The faithful support of Rome by the Smyrnians was proverbial.

Paul seems to have founded the church there during his third missionary journey (A.D. 53–57; see **Acts 19:10**). Possibly Polycarp, a pupil of John, was head of this church at this time. In A.D. 156, Polycarp was urged by the Roman authorities to say "Caesar is Lord." He refused with his famous statement, "Eighty and six years have I served Him, and He never did me any injury: how then can I blaspheme my King and my Savior?" Pressed further he finally expostulated, "You threaten me with fire that burns but for an hour, and after a little is extinguished, but are ignorant of the fire of the coming judgment and eternal punishment, reserved for the ungodly. But why delay? Bring forth what you will." Polycarp expressed in action Jesus' encouragement to Smyrna through John, **"Be faithful, even to the point of death, and I will give you the crown of life" (2:10).**

1. Jesus is the First and the Last, the everliving One who is all in all. He is the one who died and rose again for our eternal salvation and life.

2. These Christians endured poverty (unemployment), ridicule, and afflictions because of their faith. Yet they remained steadfast in their faith and profession.

3. Eventually these believers might have become so discouraged because of their persecutions that they would have given way to Satan and forsaken the Savior.

4. Possibly the encouragement to remain faithful even unto death.

5. To those who by the power of the Spirit remain faithful unto death, God would give the crown of eternal life. Such people would not be harmed by the "second death"—eternity in hell.

6. Provide students opportunity to apply this to their lives today.

PERGAMUM (Objectives 5–6)

Because of its location on a huge rocky hill overlooking a great surrounding valley, the Romans made Pergamum the capital of the province Asia. Here the god of healing, Aesculapius, was worshiped under the emblem of a serpent—for believers the very symbol of Satan. Many pagan altars, as well as the great altar to Zeus, were to be found here. As capital of the province, it was also a center for emperor worship with temples dedicated to Caesar. All Christians had to do to remain in good graces in society was to confess publicly, "Caesar is Lord," and offer a pinch of salt as a token of loyalty. Failure to do so meant loss of employment and social status, if not imprisonment and death. Some Christians reasoned, "What harm is there in doing that? We can still in our hearts worship Christ." They wanted to have it both ways—worship Christ in their hearts but worship Caesar in public.

1. Here Jesus "has the sharp, double-edged sword"—probably the Word which is a word of salvation to those who live in Christ, but a word of judgment and condemnation to those who deny or reject Him.

2. In the past these Christians had demonstrated their faithfulness to Jesus.

3. People who followed "the sin of Balaam" **(Num. 22–24)** were tolerated. These were people who wanted both God and mammon—who compromised their faith in order to be successful, or who used religion for self-gain. The sin of the Nicolaitans seems to be that of antinomianism. Professing to be Christian, they yet indulged in various immoral practices.

4. Unless the people repented of their tolerance of these people and their practices, Jesus would wield the sword of the Law—judgment and condemnation.

5. He will give "hidden manna"—Christ in all His fulness **(John 6:33, 35)**, and a "white stone"—holiness, beauty, forgiveness, and glory that will endure forever. This glory includes being identified as a child of God, and of living in close fellowship with Him forever.

6. Many applications can be given in an age in which religion is often used for self-gain, and Christians seek to be identified with God and yet pursue self-fulfillment regardless of the divine will.

THYATIRA (Objectives 5–6)

Situated in a valley connecting two other valleys, this city lacked natural fortifications and therefore was vulnerable to attack. The Romans maintained a strong military base in this city both to defend the city, and to obstruct the path of those who might seek to follow this easy route to attack the provincial capital, Pergamum. Thyatira was also a center of trade. In view of its character as an army post and a commercial city, vice and immorality were rampant—a constant temptation to the Christian who lived there.

1. Jesus' "eyes are like blazing fire"—His righteous indignation because of what He in His omniscience knows to be amiss. His "feet are like burnished bronze"—He would stamp out all enemies of the truth.

2. Jesus noted their deeds, love, faith, service, and perseverance—and the fact that they improved since they first came to faith.

3. The tendency was to "go with the flow" in order to avoid appearing to be different from their neighbors and also to indulge their sinful desires. "Whatever you believe is as good as any other person's beliefs." "Whatever feels good, do it."

4. This entire section **(2:20–28)** is an obvious call to repentance.

5. Jesus promises those who remain faithful that they will rule with Him in the age to come. They will share with Christ, the Morning Star (symbol of royalty), His royal splendor and dominion.

6. Applications in today's society are obvious.

SARDIS (Objectives 5–6)

In ancient times this city had been the capital of Lydia, but had fallen on hard times. The Romans helped it recover some of its former glory. In A.D. 17 it suffered a severe earthquake, but Tiberius helped the city rebuild. Like Thyatira, it was famous for its woolen manufactures and its dyeing industry. The ancient system of roads secured for it the trade of central Asia.

1. Jesus sends the sevenfold Spirit of God, upon whom our Christian faith and life depend, to guide and empower His church. The stars may refer to ministers of the church through whom in their teaching of the Word the Spirit works.

2. In spite of the deadness of this church, a few people still walked with Christ.

3. This church was dead. The people went through the motions of religion with its rituals, but this meant little to them.

4. **"Remember, therefore, what you have received and heard; obey it, and repent" (v. 3).**

5. Christ acknowledged the few who remained spiritually alive, and they would inherit eternal life.

6. Students will likely be able to cite examples of spiritual deadness today.

PHILADELPHIA (Objectives 5–6)

This city was founded by, and named after, Attalus II (whose devotion to his brother Eumenes gained for him the epithet "brother-lover") in 138 B.C. as a trade center for the rich volcanic region north of the city. Attalus founded Philadelphia as a center for the spread of the Greek language; therefore it had a certain "missionary" character from its beginning. It was subject to frequent earthquakes. So much of the imagery of Revelation was familiar to these people. It was a small city, so the congregation likely was quite small. Lying in a vine-growing region, the cult of Dionysus was predominant. Difficulties for Christians in this city seemed to arise more from Jewish opponents than from pagan adversaries.

1. "Holy and true" is a divine title applied to Christ, who is God. Jesus "holds the key of David"—He is the fulfillment of all the Old Testament messianic promises. He is the One who has the keys to the Kingdom; it is only through Him that a person enters the family of God.

2. In spite of their weaknesses, these Christians kept His Word and remained faithful to Him in the face of the opposition of Jews and possibly others who seem to have been Judaizers. (According to Ignatius 20 years later, the Christians in this city were more in danger from the Judaizers than the Jews.)

3. The reference to the "open door" in **3:8** suggests that these people may not have been as alive to their evangelistic opportunities as they might have.

4. John reminded the people that, in spite of their faithfulness, they too were susceptible to falling away. He warned them against a sense of false security.

5. Jesus promised to keep them safe in the hour of trial, and promised those who endured that they would be pillars in the temple of heaven in which they would dwell securely forever.

6. Students will find a variety of applications.

LAODICEA (Objectives 5–6)

Located 40 miles southeast of Philadelphia, this city was founded in the third century before Christ by Antiochus II who named it in honor of his wife Laodice. Under Roman rule it became a flourishing commercial center, noted for woolen carpets and clothing. It was a prosperous city, as is evident in **3:17–18**. This church was possibly established by Epaphras of Colossae **(Col. 1:7; 4:12–13)**. At the time of his first Roman imprisonment, Paul had not yet visited the Lycus valley **(Col. 2:1)**, but seems to have known some of the members by name **(Col. 4:15)**.

1. Here Jesus is "the faithful and true witness" who is the truth (cf., **John 3:11, 32–33; 8:14–18; 18:37; 1 Tim. 6:13**). He with the Father is the supreme ruler of all creation.

2. Really none at all. This is the only congregation of the seven in which Jesus seems to find nothing to praise.

3. The people were not only tepid in their Christianity; they were content to be so. Because of their material prosperity, they found their security and contentment in their possessions and wealth. They even boasted of their affluence.

4. It is suggested that affliction for these people

might have been helpful to refine their faith and life in God. "Gold"—genuine faith with its accompanying works. "White clothes"—life with Christ unspotted by the world. "Salve to put on your eyes" which stings but also heals—the Holy Spirit who destroys self-deception and restores spiritual vision.

5. Christ offered to enter the hearts and lives of these people to bless them and to give them the right to sit with Him on the throne of glory.

6. Applications to life today will be easy to make.

ASSIGNMENT

Here are two suggested assignments for your students.

1. Before the next session read carefully **Rev. 4:1–5:14.**

2. Once again review **Rev. 2:1–3:21** for applications to your personal life to prepare you to receive the visions you will be studying.

33. Setting the Stage

BIBLE BASIS
Rev. 4:1–5:14

CENTRAL TRUTH
Because of His redemptive life and work, Jesus now is the Mediator through whom we can approach the very throne of God.

OBJECTIVES
That the students by the power of the Spirit will
1. affirm the significance that the setting of **Revelation 4–5** has for a proper understanding of the book of **Revelation;**
2. describe the scene before the throne of God and the significance of the various persons, objects, events, and symbols found in this scene;
3. identify similarities between the scene in **Revelation 4** and **Ezekiel 1;**
4. compare the hymn of **Rev. 4:8** with similar hymns in Scripture;
5. compare the symbolic language used in **Revelation 4** with that used in other portions of Scripture;
6. describe the scroll and its significance;
7. describe the significance of the Lamb; and
8. affirm a desire to worship the Lamb in a thoughtful, meaningful manner.

BACKGROUND
The inaugural vision before the throne of God in **Revelation 4–5** sets the tone for the entire book. Several thoughts are to be accented.

1. God on His throne rules all things. He controls everything for the welfare of the church so that she may accomplish the purposes for which God established her. He also blesses the Gospel wherever it is proclaimed. This is a source of comfort for us in times of trial, and an encouragement to be faithful in sharing the Word.

2. Christ at the right hand of the Father dominates all of the book of **Revelation.**

3. In these chapters we view the ascension of Jesus as viewed from heaven. It was the coronation of Jesus to rule all things with the Father.

4. The foundation of all of **Revelation** is the sacrificial, saving life, suffering, death, and resurrection of Jesus Christ.

5. The heart of all of **Revelation** is the exalted reign of Christ. The prophecies of **Revelation** per se begin with **chapter 6.**

SETTING THE STAGE (Rev. 4:1–5)
(Objective 1)

Use these introductory paragraphs to introduce the session.

BEFORE THE THRONE OF GOD
(Objectives 2–3)

Before the session thoroughly digest the material given in this section of the student guide so that you will be able to lead the presentation and discussion fluently. Because of the nature of the material, most of this section is expository.

Encourage the students to compare the description of the four living creatures in **chapter 4** with the description of the cherubim in **Ezekiel 1** and **10** Following are some of the similarities.

1. **Rev. 4:3/Ezek. 1:28**—In both cases a rainbow encircles the throne with which the "living creatures" are associated.

2. **Rev. 4:5/Ezek. 1:13**—In both cases fire is associated with "living creatures."

3. **Rev. 4:6/Ezek. 1:5**—In both cases the symbolic number (four) is the same, and in both the beings around the throne are called "living creatures."

4. **Rev. 4:6/Ezek. 1:26**—In both cases the "living beings" are closely associated with the throne.

5. **Rev. 4:7/Ezek. 1:10**—In both cases the appearance of their faces is compared to that of man, lion, ox, and eagle.

6. **Rev. 4:8/Ezek. 1:18; 10:12**—In both cases the "living creatures" are studded all over with eyes.

OUR UNENDING HYMN (Objective 4)

1. Have students compare the Bible references provided. Offer opportunity for discussion.

a. **Matt. 21:9** tells of the Palm Sunday crowd praising Jesus with the words, "Hosanna in the highest." Jesus deserves and receives the highest form of praise. He receives this praise continuously in heaven.

b. **Is. 6:3**—Both words of praise include, "Holy, holy, holy." The repetition underscores God's complete holiness.

c. Portions of both **Matt. 21:9** and **Rev. 4:8, 11** are included in the liturgy.

2. The God who gave us life sent His Son to offer us new life through Him. Our redemption was something only God could accomplish.

THE BIBLE IN REVELATION (Objective 5)

Lead the students in a comparison of at least three of the parallel passages given. One purpose is to lead students to an understanding of the unity and interrelatedness of all parts of the Bible—the Old Testament as well as the New. What John saw by revelation is the fulfillment of the promises in the Old Testament as well as in the New.

THE OPENING OF THE SCROLL (Objective 6)

Present in your own words and style the material in the student book. Have students do the activity suggested.

THE LAMB (Objective 7)

Lead students in a comparison of **Rev. 5:6–7** with **Isaiah 53** and **Jer. 11:19**.

1. **Isaiah 53** and **Jer. 11:19** are messianic; they point to the Messiah who would redeem His people through His sacrificial life, suffering, and death. These many promises were fulfilled in Jesus Christ. Having completed His suffering and death in behalf of all people, He has now ascended to His throne to rule all things with the Father.

2. The horn is the symbol of strength **(Deut. 33:17)** or of force **(Dan. 7:7 ff.; Zech. 1:18)**. The seven horns indicate the fulness of the Lamb's power as the victorious Christ. He also possesses fulness of vision symbolized by the seven eyes. The "seven spirits of God" is the Holy Spirit whom Christ sends into the world to bring people to saving faith and to sustain believers in that faith.

3. His crucifixion.

4. To enlighten people now living in spiritual darkness so that they might walk in the light, Jesus Christ.

THE WORSHIP OF THE LAMB (Objective 8)

1. a. Jesus was slain. With His blood Jesus purchased people for God from every tribe, language, people, and nation.

b. Jesus made all these people whom He purchased to be a kingdom and priests to serve God.

c. Jesus enabled these people not only to serve God, but to reign with Him forever.

2. This question calls for students to respond according to their personal understanding of these two sections. One obvious similarity is that in both **Rev. 5:6–14** and **Is. 52:5–10,** the Servant of the Lord (or suffering Lamb of God) is depicted as redeeming all the people of God to enable them to be His people.

3. This material about the angels is interesting. Because angels are confirmed in their eternal bliss, we tend to think of them as beings superior to human beings. But in the order of God's creation, human beings are at the apex. The angels' function is to serve human beings as well as God. They are deeply interested in human beings and the salvation which God gained for them. **Eph. 3:8–11; 1 Peter 1:10–12; Luke 15:10;** and **Heb. 1:14** describe aspects of this concern and service of the angels for the welfare of human beings. So it is not strange that also in heaven they praise God for the salvation and life He gained for humankind **(5:11–12)**.

4. Human sin affects all creation (e.g., contemporary environmental problems). The redemption accomplished by Jesus Christ brings restoration and renewal not only to the human family, but also to the entire created universe. See **Col. 1:20** and **Rom. 8:18–22**.

FOR REFLECTION (Objective 8)

These questions are designed to help students internalize and apply the truths of the day to their personal lives.

ASSIGNMENT

1. Before the next session read **Rev. 6:1–7:17**.

2. Consult a complete (exhaustive) concordance of the Bible to identify every verse that refers to *angels*. What does each of these verses say about these heavenly beings whom God created? This might be the subject of a term paper.

34. Tribulations That Are to Come First Cycle

BIBLE BASIS
Rev. 6:1–7:17

CENTRAL TRUTH
Although we may have to endure persecution and testing, we can be certain that God in Christ will keep us secure in the faith until we reach the heavenly goal.

OBJECTIVES
That the students by the power of the Spirit will

1. describe the cyclical character of the revelations given to John;
2. describe the situation immediately addressed by the opening of the seven seals;
3. identify the meaning of each of the four horsemen;
4. give one answer as to why the righteous often suffer while the wicked prosper;
5. explain the significance of the upheavals in nature and society in view of the Last Day;
6. state what the meaning of the sealing of the 144,000 means for their personal life;
7. describe their blessedness and hope as they anticipate the Last Day.

THE SEVEN SEALS
(Rev.6–7; Objective 1)
The material in this section is basic for understanding the various revelations in this book. The outline in session 31 can be used to illustrate the nature of the cycles.

THE FOUR HORSEMEN (Objectives 2–3)
Review the historical background of **Revelation** as given in the Student Book. Throughout the early centuries pagans often blamed the Christians for the problems of the world. They believed that the ancient gods were offended by the inroads of Christianity into the traditional order of things and were punishing humankind for deserting them. It was in defense of Christianity against this kind of accusation that St. Augustine wrote *The City of God* (413–26).

Lead the students in the discussion of the questions designed to give students opportunity to apply the vision to their lives.

1. Accept students responses from history and the world today of situations created by each of the Four Horsemen described in the Student Book.

2. Point out that these things are the result of sin in the world. God's desires to work the salvation of people, to bless them with His good gifts regardless of the condition in which they find themselves.

3. We, too, must live in and be part of a world plagued by sin and its consequences. However, when God takes us home we will be free of all temptations, evil, and pain.

THE FIFTH SEAL (Objective 4)
Lead the students in a discussion of the material in the Student Book. Give them opportunity to discuss their questions.

THE GREAT EARTHQUAKE (Objective 5)
Throughout the Bible the writers describe upheavals in the physical world as well as in society as consequences of human sin. Such upheavals are judgments of God on sin, and reminders that we all must appear before the judgment seat of God at the last and greatest upheaval of all—the Last Day of this age. In these upheavals Christians are reminded that this world age is transitory, and they live in anticipation of the better, perfect world gained for them by the sacrificial, saving life, death, and resurrection of Jesus Christ.

1. Have students look up the passages listed to identify the following signs of the end of the world.

a. God will destroy all that proud and arrogant man has lifted up in his idolatry (**Is. 2:12–20**).

b. There will be no escaping the punishment of the Lord (**Is. 24:4–23**).

c. In His wrath God will destroy the creation (**Is. 34:2–4**).

d. In the midst of the destruction, God will send His angels to gather the elect (**Mark 13:24–27**).

You may also want to extend the discussion to the false idealism of those who believe that people of themselves can create a perfect society in this age. Such efforts can be helpful, but ultimately they are futile. This world and all therein is passing away.

2. The people of God are to watch and pray so that they may be found faithful in the day of the coming of the Lord.

THE SEALING OF THE 144,000 (Objective 6)
Review with your students the material in this section of the Students Book. Lead them in discussion of the following Bible passages and their application to everyday life today.

1. We have the confidence that He who began a good work in us will carry it on to completion until the day of Christ Jesus (**Phil. 1:6**).

2. We have been enriched in every way in Christ. God, who is faithful, has called us into fellowship with His Son (**1 Cor. 1:4–9**).

3. We can strengthen and encourage each other

with the Word of God as Timothy encouraged the people of Thessalonica **(2 Thess. 3:1–3).**

4. God is the one who sanctifies us **(1 Thess. 5:23–24).**

5. Jesus knows those who belong to Him as a shepherd knows his sheep. He will give eternal life to those who are His and will allow no one to snatch them away from Him **(John 10:27–30).**

6. We are kept by the power of God through faith until the coming of salvation **(1 Peter 1:3–5).**

7. Because of the working of the Spirit within us, nothing will be able to separate us from the love of God in Christ Jesus, our Lord **(Rom. 8:26–39).**

THE SONG OF VICTORY (Objective 7)

Rev. 7:9–17 is one of the most familiar—and beautiful—sections of this book.

For most effective learning have students answer the questions at the end on the basis of their own searching of Scripture.

1. God's promise to Abraham was that his seed would be a great multitude which no one could number. The vision of heaven reveals to us all of the spiritual "seed" of Abraham—"a great multitude that no one could count."

2. The white robes and palms point to the homage given Jesus already in Jerusalem on Palm Sunday; He is the promised Messiah in whom our sins have been cleansed, and through whose cleansing blood we now can appear before God.

3. Both **Psalm 98** and **Rev. 7:10, 12** are songs of praise to the Savior for the salvation He gained and gives to all humankind. (Salvation is God's free gift. If we are lost, it is only because we reject that gift.)

4. We will serve God day and night in perfect happiness and bliss. We will never hunger, thirst, or experience pain or discomfort. God will wipe every tear from our eyes.

ASSIGNMENT

These are suggested assignments for your students.

1. Before the next session read **Rev. 8:1–9:21.**

2. In **Psalms** find at least three other songs that celebrate the victories of God.

35. Tribulations That Are to Come Second Cycle

BIBLE BASIS
Rev. 8:1–9:21

CENTRAL TRUTH

Although God permits Satan to seek the destruction of His created physical universe and humankind, He still rules the universe and the course of human history in His infinite power and grace.

OBJECTIVES

That the students by the power of the Spirit will

1. describe with greater understanding and clarity the nature and significance of the cycles found in **Revelation;**
2. describe the interlude that precedes and prepares for the second cycle;
3. describe the significance of the trumpet imagery found in **Revelation;**
4. note the effects of sin on the physical world as indicated by the first four trumpet blasts;
5. describe the growing warfare on humankind by Satan and his followers;
6. describe the limitations that God places on Satan's assaults on humanity and the world;
7. recognize the ebb and flow in human history of the effectiveness of Satan's attacks on, and seduction of, humankind;
8. describe the rule of God's grace in a universe in which Satan and evil seem to be supreme.

INTRODUCTION (Objective 1)

Because the cyclical structure of **Revelation** is so important for the proper understanding and interpretation of this book, use the introductory period to deepen your students' understanding of the nature and significance of these cycles. Appropriate material is given in the introduction. Additional material may be found in such commentaries on **Revelation** as that by R. C. H. Lenski.

PREPARATION FOR THE SECOND CYCLE (Objectives 2–3)

1. Incense symbolizes prayer. **Rev. 8:3–4** and **5:8** emphasize the importance and efficacy of the communion with God by God's people on earth through prayer.

2. As He rules during this period from His ascension to the Last Day, Jesus responds in His grace and wisdom to the prayers of His people on earth. As we live in a world filled with the woes of God's judgment, we have been sealed so that we might be safe, and we can commune with our Lord through prayer in the midst of the trials and tribulations that befall this world.

3. The passages below provide some clarification of the trumpet imagery.

a. **Joshua 6:1–5/Rev. 11:13**—trumpets used for ceremonial processions.

b. **1 Kings. 1:34, 39; 2 Kings. 9:13**—trumpets

blown to proclaim the accession and coronation of a king.

c. **Ps. 47:5; 98:6; Zech. 9:14; Rev. 11:15**—trumpets associated with the kingship of God.

d. **Is. 58:1; Jer. 4:5–6; 6:1, 17–19; Ezek. 33:3–9; Joel 2:1, 12–16; Rev. 9:20–21**—trumpets used as an alarm signal to summon the Israelites to national repentance in the face of imminent divine judgment.

e. **Num. 10:10 and Rev. 11:15, 18**—the trumpet used as a ritualistic reminder that God would always remember His people.

NATURE POLLUTED (Objective 4)

After introducing this section with the opening sentence, lead students in discussion of the six questions.

1. In **Rom. 8:19–22** Paul indicated that the entire physical universe suffers from the consequences of human sin. However, all of nature will be renewed when Jesus comes again to usher in the new heaven and the new earth. (Some people refer to this passage to suggest that our pets will be with us in heaven.)

2. Discuss student responses.

3. The catastrophic events in nature are signs of the end of this age, and the eventual establishment of a new heaven and a new earth which will endure forever, and which will be characterized by perfect peace and righteousness.

4. That only a fraction is destroyed with each plague indicates that this punishment is not yet complete and final. The purpose of these visitations is to warn people of the wrath and judgment of God, and to bring them to repentance and saving faith. God is patient in His grace and mercy.

5. The first set of passages speaks of darkness as a symbol of divine judgment. The second set connects darkness with the demonic.

6. Note the similarities between the plagues of Egypt and those preceding the Last Day. Both include the plague of hail (**Ex. 9:13–35/Rev. 8:7**), the turning of water into blood (**Ex. 7:14–24/Rev. 8:10**), and darkness (**Ex. 10:21–29/Rev. 8:12**).

7. The Egyptian plagues preceded the Exodus of God's people from the tyranny of Egypt to the Promised Land of Canaan. The plagues of **Revelation** precede the new Exodus of God's people from the tyranny of this sinful world to the Promised Land of the age to come.

THE ASSAULT FROM HELL
(The First Woe; Objectives 5–6)

In your own words and style, discuss with your students the material in this section.

THE RESERVES ARE BROUGHT IN
(The Second Woe; Objectives 7–8)

A summary of the contents and meanings of **Rev. 9:13–21** is given in the Student Book.

1. In **Ephesians 6** and **Romans 8** Paul wrote about the intense conflict between the people of God and the forces of evil.

a. In **Eph. 6:10–18** Paul described the battle as a spiritual one that takes place against evil "in the heavenly realms" (v. 12).

b. Our enemies are the forces of spiritual darkness—the rulers, authorities, and powers of this dark world and the spiritual forces of evil in the heavenly realms (v. 12).

c. In order to resist we must rely upon God and His protection and power; we are powerless against these foes on our own. God tells us to ready ourselves for battle by putting on His armor—the belt of truth, the breastplate of righteousness, the gospel of peace on our feet, the shield of faith, the helmet of salvation, the sword of the Spirit which is the Word of God (vv. 13–17).

d. God has the ultimate power over the forces of evil.

e. We have the promise that those who face persecution, suffering, and death, **"in all these things we are more than conquerors through Him who loved us" (Rom. 8:37).** Further, we have the assurance that **"neither angels nor demons, neither the present nor the future, nor any powers, neither height nor depth, nor anything else in all creation, will be able to separate us from the love of God that is in Christ Jesus our Lord" (Rom. 8:38–39).**

2. Discuss student responses.

3. By God's grace the church continues to teach the Word and administer the Sacraments unhindered in many parts of the world. The church continues to grow even in those places where those who follow Christ are most severely persecuted.

4. We are part of the church. It is our privilege and obligation to reach out to others with the saving Gospel as God opens doors for us. Ask students for examples of how God has used them to share to Good News with someone else.

ASSIGNMENT

These are some suggested student assignments.

1. Before the next session read **Rev. 10:1–11:19**.

2. Consult Bible reference books (e.g., dictionary, commentary) to ascertain the significance of the following items for Old Testament believers: cloud and rainbow (**10:1**), the temple (**11:1**), sackcloth (**11:3**), ark of the covenant (**11:19**).

36. What's a Nice Person Like You Doing in This Kind of World?

BIBLE BASIS
   Rev. 10:1–11:19

CENTRAL TRUTH

As God calls His people to share the Gospel of Jesus Christ in the face of opposition and hostility, He provides us with His presence and strength so that we may fulfill our mission with confident joy and hope.

OBJECTIVES

That the students by the power of the Spirit will

1. describe at least two purposes for which God has placed them in this world filled with so much evil;
2. identify the Mighty One who has called them into mission;
3. point out why they can fulfill their mission in confidence;
4. give personal evidence that they understand why they can anticipate opposition and hostility as they seek to fulfill their God-given mission; and
5. explain why they can look toward the future, especially the end of their lives and of this world, with eager anticipation and joy.

INTRODUCTION (Objective 1)

In this vision of the seven trumpets John saw that which is to occur in church and society between the Lord's ascension and the Last Day. Throughout the entire New Testament era God's people can expect to endure along with the world the results of sin in the form of calamities and death. In addition, Christians can expect to suffer just because they are Christian. Here John prepares the people of God for the tribulations to come and gives them the assurance that the living Jesus will be with them to sustain and support them, and finally receive them into eternal bliss with Him at the throne of heaven.

THE ONE WHO CALLS US (Objective 2)

Some believe the "mighty angel" (**10:1**) is Jesus Himself. Having a face like the sun and a rainbow on the head as well as being robed in a cloud indicates this being is either Christ, the Son of Man, or he may be an angel closely associated with Him for the fulfilling of His will.

1. The appearance of the angel and his mission to call John (and all Christians) to proclaim to humankind the revelation of God is similar to the appearance of the being who called Ezekiel to bring the message of the Lord to rebellious Israel (**Rev. 10:1–3/Ezek. 1:26–2:5**).

2. The cloud symbolizes the judgment of God on humankind as well as His majesty as He speaks through His Word. (The angel's face like the sun denotes holiness.)

3. The rainbow points to God's covenant of grace in Jesus Christ with His people.

4. The fiery pillars would remind John's readers of the pillar of fire by which God led the Israelites during the Exodus. So God continues to lead His people as they travel the road of the Exodus from the evil of this age to the eternal holiness and glory in heaven.

5. The voice from heaven in **10:4** likely was that of God, who commissioned John (and all witnesses in every age) to proclaim that which was being revealed to him—especially the saving Gospel of Jesus Christ. The placing of the right foot on the sea and the left foot on the land indicates His message given through John is for the entire world. It must be heard by all, for this message of God will dominate all history. This is why God has also placed us in the world today. God has called us for this mission, even as he called John in **Revelation**. This figure also emphasizes God's authority over all that exists.

THE PURPOSE AND TASK FOR WHICH WE ARE CALLED (Objective 1)

In your own way share the contents of the narrative material in the Student Book.

1. Like Ezekiel, John was to eat the scroll and then prophesy before or about many peoples, nations, languages, and kings. This is the church's missionary charter. Compare the charge to Ezekiel with that to John in **Rev. 10:7–11**.

2. To read and internalize this message. As the Collect for the Word has it, "Blessed Lord, who hast caused all Holy Scriptures to be written for our learning, grant that we may in such wise hear them, read, mark, learn, and *inwardly digest them,* that by patience and comfort of Thy holy Word we may embrace, and ever hold fast, the blessed hope of everlasting life, which Thou hast given us in our Savior Jesus Christ" (*The Lutheran Hymnal,* p. 14). "Eat"—complete appropriation to the receiver of prophetic revelation before communicating it to others.

3. "Sweet"—joy in the promises of God. The Gospel of Jesus Christ itself is sweet and glorious. But the scroll also contains a word of judgment; its proclamation is often followed by bitter persecution.

4. Having appropriated the Word of God, John (and we) are to proclaim it to all people before the end of this age.

5. Give students time to verbalize how they today might fulfill their purpose in this world as Christians.

CONFIDENCE TO CONFESS BOLDLY (Objective 3)

Lead the students in a discussion of the material in this section of the Student Book.

GATHERING CLOUDS (Objective 4)

One would think that people in their hopeless situation would be eager to become a person of God by His free grace. But the contrary is usually true.

1 and 2. When the period allotted for the Gospel proclamation is over, Satan will be released from bondage just before the end of the world. With all the anti-Christian forces in the world and from hell, he will do his best to battle against the church and destroy it. This is the Battle of Armageddon that will occur for a brief period just before the Last Day (see **Rev. 20:7–9**).

The "beast" is all forms of tyranny. Tyrants who seek to master and use other people for their sinful purposes will come in many forms in government, education, industry, culture, communications, and other forms of human endeavor.

For John the "great city" was probably Rome with its worldwide empire and emperor worship. At other points in history it has been Egypt, Babylon, Assyria, and more recently, Berlin under Hitler and Moscow under men such as Stalin.

3. As a result of this onslaught, the church as a definable, witnessing community will be destroyed—or go underground as seems to have happened in China and Russia. During these periods of intense persecutions, the church will be dead, ineffectual. **Rev. 11:9–10** depicts the hatred of the pagan world for Christians and the joy in which unbelievers receive the opposition against Christians. One example today is that people who want to live in sin, and so many do happily, refuse to go to church because the Word of God condemns them. They are not ready to repent and place their trust in Christ.

4. Through human history there has been an ebb and flow in the fortunes of Christianity. Periods of persecution and depression have been followed by times of outstanding growth. At the last, the Battle of Armageddon will be followed by the return of Christ to inaugurate the eternal time of glory for all His people from every age to rule together forever. **Ezek. 37:4–14** speaks of the breath of life that the Spirit gave the dead bones, which is symbolic of the life that the Holy Spirit gives even today.

THE DAY OF TRIUMPH (Objective 5)

The seventh trumpet sounds. For unbelievers this is the sound of judgment and eternal torment and death. Justice is served.

But for the people of God who placed their trust for life and salvation not in themselves and their works, but in the saving life and work of Jesus Christ, the blast of the seventh trumpet announces the beginning of eternal glory. This is a fine positive note on which to end the session.

ASSIGNMENT

The following are suggested activities for students prior to the next .

1. In preparation for the next session read **Revelation 12–14;** give special attention to **chapter 12.**
2. With the help of a concordance look up the passages that deal with the tribulations and persecutions to be expected by believers because of their faith. For each passage ask: What is the cause for such opposition? What assurance does God give His people for such times?

37. The Gathering Storm

BIBLE BASIS
Rev. 12:1–17

CENTRAL TRUTH

Although Satan uses every possible means to destroy the church, God in Christ will enable His people to remain faithful even during times of hostility and opposition.

OBJECTIVES

That the students by the power of the Spirit will

1. describe the purpose of the interlude between the visions of the seven seals **(Rev. 6:1–8:5)** and the seven trumpets **(Rev. 8:6–11:19)** and that of the seven bowls **(15:1–16:21);**
2. identify the causes behind the outward struggle between the church and the world;
3. explain the symbolism and meaning of the vision of the dragon, woman, and child;
4. describe the significance of the war in heaven; and
5. express the joy and confidence Christians can experience in the midst of opposition and hostility.

INTRODUCTION (Objectives 1–2)

Use the introductory material in the Student Book to lay a foundation for the day's session.

DRAGON, WOMAN, AND CHILD (Objectives 2–3)

This is a very long section. You may wish to ask students to prepare in advance for the discussion. The exposition and Bible passages cited in the Student Book are quite clear. However, the following identification of the symbolism may be helpful.

1. Scene—heaven. From the perspective of

heaven the church is glorious, but from the perspective of earth it is taunted and miserable.

a. Sign—a great spectacle that points to the consummation of all earthly things. Jesus has told us that the Last Day will be preceded by great earthquakes, famines, pestilences in various places, fearful events and great signs from heaven, signs in the sun, moon, and stars, nations in anguish and perplexity at the roaring and tossing of the sea, wonders in the heaven above and signs on the earth below, blood and fire and billows of smoke **(Luke 21:11, 25; Acts 2:19).**

b. Woman—the church **(Gal. 4:21–31/Is. 54:1).**

c. Garment of the sun—although despised by the world, from God's point of view the church is radiant, glorious, and exalted.

The moon underneath the woman's feet—the church exercises dominion.

The crown of 12 stars—the royalty of the church. The 12 stars represent the people of God (12 tribes of Israel; 12 apostles).

d. Cries—birth pangs **(Gen. 3:15–16; Is. 66:7).**

Child—the Seed of the woman, will defeat Satan **(Gen. 3:15),** will be God with us **(Is. 7:14),** will be called **"Wonderful Counselor, Mighty God, Everlasting Father, Prince of Peace" (Is. 9:6).** He will reign with power and might **(Ps. 2:9)** and He is the Son of God, **"born of a woman, born under law, to redeem those under law, that we might receive the full rights of sons" (Gal. 4:4–5).**

e. Dragon—the serpent called Satan **(12:9; 20:2).**

Red—the destructive character of Satan.

2. Not content with being creatures of God, certain angels wanted to be as God. They rebelled against Him to establish their own independence.

a. When these angels sinned, God condemned them to hell **(2 Peter 2:4).**

b. These force of evil continue to battle against the people of God **(Eph. 6:12).**

c. God has kept the angels who rebelled against Him in darkness, **"bound with everlasting chains for judgment on the great Day" (Jude 6).**

d. Our enemy, the devil, has always been and will always continue to be a murderer and a liar **(John 8:44).**

e. Sinners are the servant of the devil, but Jesus came to destroy the work of the devil **(1 John 3:8).**

3. The woman (church) continues to live in this world subject to Satan's temptations. But God has prepared a refuge **(the desert, v. 6)** for the people of God. The stay in the desert represents the period of the present age during which the people of God, surrounded by God's enemies, witness to the salvation in Jesus.

a. The desert would have reminded John's readers of the desert in which the children of Israel lived for 40 years on their way to the Promised Land **(Ex. 16:1, 10).** Here, God fed them with food from heaven, and provided that their clothes did not wear out and their feet did not swell **(Deut. 8:2–5).** Also, God provided for Elijah as he stayed by the brook in the Kerith Ravine through the ravens who brought Elijah bread and meat **(1 Kings 17:2–6).** Another time when Elijah fled into the desert in order to escape Jezebel, God sent His angel to strengthen him **(1 Kings 19:2–9).**

Perhaps John's reader were also reminded of the flight of Mary, Joseph, and the baby Jesus to Egypt **(Matt. 2:13–15)** or of Hosea's leading of his wife into the desert to comfort and encourage her **(Hos. 2:14–15).**

b. God's people have assurances of safety in this "desert" of refuge. Through the Word of God we have the saving knowledge of all that God in Christ has done for us. Plus we enjoy the fellowship of others who trust in Jesus **(1 John 1:3),** and the grace and peace of our Lord, the love of God, and the fellowship of the Holy Spirit **(2 Cor. 13:11–14).**

WAR IN HEAVEN (Objective 4)

Examples of Satan using the Law to accuse the people of God can be found in the account of Job **(Job 1:6–12).** Satan stated that Job worshiped God only because of the material rewards he had received in return for his devotion. **Zech. 3:1–5** pictures Satan before God accusing Joshua of having fallen short of God's standards. Joshua was able to stand because the Lord had taken away his sin **(3:5),** not because of Joshua's perfection.

1. In **Dan. 12:1–4,** Michael is presented as the guardian of Israel who protects God's people from the attacks and accusations of Satan. He intercedes for God's people against Satan **(Jude 9).** The function of Michael is to help, support, and protect the people of God **(Dan. 10:13, 21; 12:1).** In both **Dan. 12:1–4** and **Rev. 12:7–12** we see Michael fighting against Satan to defend God's people from his attacks and to deliver them safely into heaven at the end.

2. **Rev. 12:9–12** is a beautiful description of our protection against Satan and the sure hope of eternal life with God that we have through the saving life, death, and resurrection of Jesus Christ. But this hymn also includes a most solemn warning to those on earth against the determined efforts of Satan to destroy them. In Romans 8 Paul also confesses unequivocally that Satan cannot rightly bring any charge or condemnation against God's people because Christians are secure in the protecting grace of God.

WAR ON EARTH (Objective 5)

Christians in the world will continue to be attacked by Satan, but God carries the church into the wilderness—into the place of refuge and security from Satan's attacks.

1. Even as God delivered His people from the tyranny of the Egyptians by carrying them "on eagle's wings" into the wilderness near Sinai to protect them, so He carries His people today "on eagle's wings" to

liberate them from the tyranny of the devil.

2. In **Gen. 3:15** God said there would be enmity between the devil and the woman as well as her seed (offspring).

3. Summarize the session by giving students opportunity to identify some of the problems they might expect because of their allegiance to Christ, but also the joys and confidence they have in God.

ASSIGNMENT

Some suggested assignments are as follows:
1. Before the next session read **Rev. 13:1–14:20**.
2. In various Bible references discover what you can about the archangel Michael.

38. The War Intensifies

BIBLE BASIS
Rev. 13:1–14:20

CENTRAL TRUTH
God, in His power and grace, allows those who trust in Him to live victorious over the powerful forces of evil around them which are bent upon destroying their souls.

OBJECTIVES
That the students by the power of the Spirit will

1. describe the cyclical nature of the predominance of either good or evil in human history;
2. describe how Satan establishes and uses tyrannical political powers to serve as his tools in order to accomplish his deceptive and destructive goals;
3. describe how anti-Christian philosophies and religions seek the destruction of human souls;
4. describe the mission of the three angels;
5. describe the warning and the reassurance they received from this session; and
6. praise God for His power and grace that enables them to live victoriously.

INTRODUCTION (Objective 1)
On the basis of the material in the Student Book describe how in human history periods of warfare and peace, depression and prosperity, seem to alternate. When it appears that we have fairly well solved our problems of poverty and conflict, therefore becoming optimistic concerning the future, new waves of conflict and oppression appear.

The introduction alludes to examples in the 20th century of this cyclical nature of history. You can reach back into past centuries. For example, at the time of John the Roman Empire covered most of Western Europe, the Near East, and northern Africa. Universal peace prevailed for the most part. Within centuries the centers of power shifted to Constantinople and to northern Europe. The Dark Ages followed the classical period of John's time. Thus there is an ebb and flow to the fortunes of nations and peoples.

THE BEAST FROM THE SEA (Objective 2)
Revelation 13 shows us the instruments that the dragon (Satan) uses for his attack on the people of God.

In your own way present the material in the Student Book.

1. Similarities between **Dan. 7:1–25** and **Rev. 13:1–10** include, among others, the following items:

a. Daniel saw four great beasts arise from the sea (**Dan. 7:3**). The beast of **Revelation** also emerged from the sea (**13:1**).

b. The four beasts of **Daniel** were like a lion, an eagle, a bear, and a leopard (**7:4–6**). In **Revelation**, **"the beast I saw resembled a leopard, but had feet like those of a bear and a mouth like that of a lion"** (**13:2**).

c. The fourth beast of **Daniel** (**7:7**) had ten horns. The beast of **Revelation** also had ten horns (**13:1**).

Other similarities can be noted.

2. A comparison of the imagery of **Revelation 13** and other sections of the Bible is as follows.

a. In both **Rev. 13:1** and **Is. 17:12** the *sea* represents the violent character of nations and political forces.

b. *Leopard* represents swiftness, cunning; it is large and fierce, swift to spring upon its prey.

c. A *bear* is ready to rend and tear, eager with its great and terrible feet to crush the enemy.

d. The growling and roaring *lion,* eager to have its prey, is anxious to destroy. You may wish to spend more time in discussing the appropriateness of these images as used in Scripture.

3. Some Biblical examples are Assyria, Babylonia, the Greece of Alexander the Great, Syria, Egypt, and Rome. Located at the crossroads of the ancient world, Palestine was always vulnerable to the marching armies of the great powers. John was most likely thinking of Rome.

4. This is a discussion question to provide opportunity for application. One notable example would be Russia. It is interesting that in Russia—and China—the church has continued in spite of intense persecution. It went into hiding, to be sure, but it has emerged perhaps stronger than ever.

5. Answers will vary.

6. One purpose is to bring people to repentance and faith. God's people may wander from Him. God permits affliction to fall in order to bring them back.

7 and 8. The passages cited are clear; the questions are designed for open discussion.

THE BEAST OUT OF THE EARTH (Objective 3)

Present the material in the Student Book to your class. The questions are designed for discussion and application.

1. Secular humanism is but one example of the second beast, although it may appear harmless enough—even beneficial—for everyone, including the people of God. This philosophy displaces God from His rightful position and is therefore idolatrous. Other examples include the New Age movement, Satanism, Communism, etc.

2. Persons in government and politics can use Christianity to effect their own personal advancement.

3. Since the digit 6 refers to man, the repetition of 6 in the number 666 most likely represents the glorification of man and the forces of evil. Its repetition also points to the failures of human governments throughout history to resolve the problems and consequences of sin.

THE TRIUMPH OF THE SAINTS (Objective 6)

The material in the Student Book is self-explanatory. In **Ps. 125:1–2**, Mt. Zion stands for the church, the people of God, and emphasizes that the church cannot be destroyed because it is eternal and is surrounded by the protecting power of God.

THE MISSION OF THE ANGELS (Objective 4)

Most of the material in this section is self-explanatory. Have the students discuss the questions at the conclusion of the section.

1. **Luke 17:26–30** suggests that many people are lost because in this life they are so preoccupied with everyday activities that they ignore God and their eternal welfare.

2. Examples of indifference to warnings of judgment and the Gospel include materialism, disrespect for God's Word and the holy ministry, declines in church membership, preoccupation with self-satisfaction. Poor Bible study habits, "Sunday" Christianity, lack of zeal for mission work, and poor stewardship all indicate complacency on the part of the people of God. This spirit can be overcome only by the power of the Spirit of God, who works in human hearts through Word and sacraments.

3. Answers will include times students reached out with the Word of God especially to those who in their absorption with the challenges and charms of this world are unconcerned and indifferent about their future and eternal well-being.

4. "Babylon" might well be the country, city, or section of the community in which your students live.

5. It is difficult to endure patiently, obey God's commandments, and remain faithful to Jesus because the temptations around us are so great. Opinions may vary as to whether it is more difficult today to persevere than in former ages.

THE FINAL HARVEST (Objectives 5–6)

1. In this age God permits the weeds to grow with the grain. However, at the end of this world in His divine and final judgement God will separate the weeds from the grain. Both **Rev. 14:14–20** and **Matt. 13:24–30** tell of this.

2. Both **Dan. 7:13–14** and **Rev. 14:14** speak of Jesus as the Son of Man, a term Jesus preferred using when referring to Himself. In both passages the Son of Man comes on the clouds of heaven to judge and to receive universal and lasting dominion. The white cloud denotes holiness, the crown points to Him as the Messiah who has conquered and thereby earned the right to act in judgment. The sharp sickle is the instrument of harvest and depicts the Son of Man as coming to harvest the earth in judgment.

3. Give students opportunity to respond to this question.

ASSIGNMENT

Encourage students to do these activities before the next session.

1. Read **Rev. 15:1–16:21**.

2. Prepare a report on the concept of the Son of Man in Scripture. Use a concordance and other appropriate Bible reference books.

39. Tribulations That Are to Come Third Cycle

BIBLE BASIS
Rev. 15:1–16:21

CENTRAL TRUTH

Through human history and events, as well as through phenomena in the world of nature, God preserves and protects those who belong to Him through Christ as He pronounces judgment upon those who oppose Him and oppress His people.

OBJECTIVES

That the students by the power of the Spirit will

1. explain why Christians can rejoice in the midst of those tribulations which God permits to befall the world as the consequences of human sin;
2. describe the glorious state of the saints in heaven;
3. tell how God uses disorders in nature to punish the enemies of His people;
4. recognize how God also uses political disorders for

judgment on those who oppose Him and oppress His people; and
5. identify the message of hope all Christians have in the midst of living in a decaying world.

INTRODUCTION (Objective 1)

It is good to review once again the cyclical structure of **Revelation** as an introduction to the third cycle. Each cycle begins with the ascension of Christ and depicts the history and trial of the church from that day to the Second Coming of Christ. However, each cycle approaches this history from a somewhat different perspective. The third and final cycle emphasizes the final judgments to be poured out on humankind.

THE CHURCH TRIUMPHANT (Objective 2)

1. The previous sign **(Rev. 12:1–3)** was the woman, the church. The whole history of the church has been one of conflict between the Seed of the woman (the Savior, cf. **Gen. 3:15**) and Satan and his followers. The sign of **Revelation 15** is the final evil that the oppressors of God's people will experience as God's judgments before the Last Day. These plagues belong to the drama of the continuing conflict between the church and the world.

2. A close connection exists between the sea of **Revelation 15** and the sea of **Exodus 14**. In both cases it is used for the judgments of God upon the wicked who oppress His people. Even as the oppressors of the Israelites were punished by means of the Red Sea in **Exodus 14**, so through the sea of glass will the believers of all eras be avenged. In the exodus as well as in the mission of Jesus we see the victory of the Lamb.

3. All believers who endure faithfully in spite of persecution.

4. In both cases (deliverance of the Israelites at the Red Sea and deliverance of humanity through the sacrificial life, suffering, death, and resurrection of Jesus Christ) it was the Lamb who gave the victory.

5. During the exodus, God dwelt within the tabernacle with its ark of the covenant. This figure is used here to point out that the seven bowls are *God's* judgment on the unbelieving world.

6. Smoke is the Old Testament symbol of the divine presence when the awe and majesty of the just and righteous God is being emphasized. It refers to the full and thorough operation of God's righteous wrath.

7. The gold indicates the bowls are to be used for God's purposes. The bowls are full to indicate the fierceness and unmitigated character of God's wrath.

It is everlasting wrath for it proceeds from the eternal God. This judgment is final and one that will endure throughout eternity.

PLAGUES OF NATURE (Objective 3)

1. Aspects of nature affected by the first four plagues include physical health, earth, salt water, fresh water, and the sun.

2. Both **Rev. 16:1–9** and **Matt. 24:29–31** emphasize that catastrophes in the physical universe will be a sign that this age is passing away, and that the Lord will return to make all things new.

3. God's enemies will suffer almost unbelievably while His people will enjoy eternal, perfect joy and bliss.

4. Many answers can be given. One is that the patient bearing of burdens is a testimony to the power and comfort of the Gospel in the believer's life.

5. This question is for application to personal life.

PLAGUES AMONG THE NATIONS (Objective 4)

Read and discuss this section with your students.

THE END OF ALL THINGS (Objective 5)

1. a. Great voices in heaven proclaim the realization of the kingdom of God **(11:15)**; a great voice from the heavenly temple declares that God's purpose has been accomplished **(16:17)**.

b. The 24 elders announce the arrival of the time of judgment **(11:18)**; judgment falls on the entire earth **(16:19–20)**.

c. In **Rev. 11:19–21** we read that the heavenly temple of God is opened, and there are lightnings, voices, thunders, and earthquake and hail; in **Rev. 16:18, 21** we read that there are lightnings, voices, thunders, and the greatest of all earthquakes and tremendous hail. Note the similarity in the way God's judgments are depicted **(16:18, 21)**.

2. An open question for observation and discussion.

3. In spite of all the evidences of God's judgment on sin, many unbelievers persist in their unbelief and evil ways.

4. A discussion question for personal application.

ASSIGNMENT

Suggested assignments are as follows:
1. Read **Rev. 17:1–18:24**.
2. In a complete Bible concordance identify all passages listed under "hail" and/or "earthquake." Look up the passages in the Bible. Which passages speak of these phenomena as judgments of God?

40. The Fall of Babylon

BIBLE BASIS
Rev. 17:1–18:24

CENTRAL TRUTH

Although God in His grace and mercy continues to delay His coming in judgment in order to give all people ample opportunity to repent and believe the Gospel, He assuredly will come eventually to judge and condemn all those who persist in their unbelief and to inaugurate a new age for those who come to faith in Christ.

OBJECTIVES

That the students by the power of the Spirit will

1. identify the great harlot in **Revelation 17–18**;
2. identify Babylon as used in **Revelation 17–18**;
3. describe how people often substitute political powers and human government for God;
4. explain why wars to overcome tyranny are never completely and finally successful;
5. describe why Christians can live in quiet confidence even in the midst of oppression by anti-Christian political powers and religious forces; and
6. explain why it is important for a person to trust and worship God even though it may seem to be more profitable to seek one's good in human agencies.

INTRODUCTION

Use material in the introduction in the Student Book to introduce students to the session.

MORE ABOUT BABYLON (Objectives 1–3)

In **Rev. 17:1–2** the "great prostitute" seems to represent the influence of all false religions, and especially false Christianity, opposed to the reality that we are justified before God by His grace in Jesus Christ alone. During the Middle Ages the organized church itself often fitted this description. Even today all religions and religious teachers who lead people away from trust in Jesus Christ alone for salvation to faith in themselves or in other persons and agencies would be "great prostitutes." The prostitute seated on the beast represents tyrannical political powers as well as false religions that oppose believers in Jesus Christ.

In John's day, the "many waters" of **Rev. 17:1, 15** represented all the teeming, mixed peoples of the Roman Empire. In any age the "waters" would represent peoples governed by tyrannical political powers and false religious forces.

THE MYSTERY OF BABYLON REVEALED (Objectives 1, 2, and 4)

Present this material to your students. The questions at the end of the section are designed for open discussion and application.

1. Possible answers include many of the political forces in the world today.

2. Evil will continue in one form or another until the end of time. Wars are sometimes necessary to protect the freedom of ourselves and others.

3. Answers include religions that have the form of Christianity but deprive people of the Gospel. Many of the contemporary cults are examples.

4. Seductive influences exist wherever one resides.

5. A successful person is one who has received the gift of salvation and lives a life of faith, endeavoring to share this greatest of gifts with others.

6. We must exercise care to not fall under the influence of all that would seek to turn our hearts away from God and His free gift of salvation in Christ Jesus.

7. This wisdom is the gift of the Holy Spirit made available to the people of God through Word and sacraments.

ANNOUNCEMENT IN HEAVEN CONCERNING THE DOOM OF BABYLON (Objective 5)

1. The words used by Isaiah to announce the fall of ancient Babylon by Cyrus **(Is. 21:8–10)** are also used to announce the fall of the Babylon of John's day (Rome) and all "Babylons" in human history **(Rev. 18:1–3)**. In both **Is. 13:19–22** and **Rev. 18:1–3**, Babylon upon its fall will be left desolate, a haunt for wild beasts.

2. Unfaithfulness to God and the pursuit of wealth and luxuries led to Rome's fall. Many contemporary applications will be easy to find.

3. In the midst of the unfaithfulness of "Babylon," messengers of God appear among the people to seek their repentance and their return to God.

4. To depart from Babylon means that God's people are not to partake of its unbelief and sins. Discuss the similarities between **Rev. 18:5–8** and the following passages.

a. In **Is. 48:20–22** God tells His people to flee the Babylonians. He says He has redeemed his servant Jacob, but that there is no peace for the wicked.

b. In **Jer. 50:8–10** God tells His people to come out of Babylon because Babylon will be attacked, captured, and plundered.

c. **Zech. 2:7–9** records God's judgment against all who would touch the "apple of His eye." God promises to come soon to live among His people.

d. **Is. 52:11–12** tells of God's command for His people to depart and touch no unclean thing. God promises to go before His people and behind them for protection.

e. **Jer. 51:54–57** announces God's intent to destroy Babylon.

f. In **2 Cor. 6:16–18** God tells His people to separate themselves from evil. He promises to be as a Father to His people.

In one way or another, all of these passages speak of Babylon's predetermined downfall, warning God's people to flee from the city and its ways lest they too be destroyed with the city. These passages emphasize that God is the one who redeems, protects, and delivers His people. Today we tend to trust in human beings and institutions for our good. But all of these will eventually be destroyed. The only lasting foundation for one's life is the grace of God in Jesus Christ.

5. All material possessions must one day pass away from our grasp.

THE EARTH'S LAMENT (Objective 6)

1. Both passages speak of the destruction of all things and the futility of placing one's ultimate trust in this material world.

2. The rising smoke announces the destruction of Babylon by fire. In Scripture the imagery of fire is prominent in the description of the collapse of this world order as the Last Day approaches.

3 and 4. Discussion questions.

5. Not because they delight in the destruction of other people, but because this announces the end of all persecution and oppression.

THE FINAL MILLSTONE FROM HEAVEN (Objective 6)

1. When they see that God's promise that this world will one day end does not seem to be fulfilled, many people feel that this world will always go on and that they need not repent and believe the Gospel. Yet, God delays His coming to give people added opportunities to come to a saving relationship with Him. But we can be assured that this age *will* finally end, and that we will be raised to a perfect, eternal life in the age to come.

2. **2 Peter 3:11–18** shares many ways in which God's people are to anticipate the Last Day. Some of these are as follows.

The people of God are to live holy and godly lives as they look forward to the day of God and speed its coming **(vv. 11–12)**; look forward to a new heaven and a new earth, the home of righteousness **(v. 13)**; make every effort to be found spotless, blameless, at peace with God, and patient **(vv. 14–15)**; be on guard so that we may not be carried away by the error of lawless men and fall from our secure position, but rather grow in the grace and knowledge of our Lord and Savior Jesus Christ **(v. 17–18)**.

ASSIGNMENT

You may wish to assign these activities to your students.

1. Before the next session read **Rev. 19:1–21**.

2. Gather material on the various forms of millennialism (amillennialism; premillennialism; postmillennialism).

41. The Victory Celebration

BIBLE BASIS
Rev. 19:1–21

CENTRAL TRUTH
In the visions of the marriage of the Lamb and the rider on the white horse, Christians in every age are assured of Christ's final victory over all evil—a victory He shares with all His faithful followers.

OBJECTIVES
That the students by the power of the Spirit will

1. express joy in the future that they have in Jesus Christ;
2. praise God for His victory over all evil forces that seek to destroy God's people;
3. describe how the period from the time of Christ on earth to the Last day can be compared to ancient Jewish wedding customs;
4. describe and explain the significance of the vision of the rider on the white horse; and
5. express personal assurance derived from the visions reported in **Revelation 19**.

INTRODUCTION (Objective 1)
Use material in the Student Book to introduce the session.

THE VICTORY SONG (Objective 2)
1 and 2. In **19:1–4** the multitudes of angels join in praising God, who in judging and condemning the great harlot has perfected the salvation of His people. It is God alone who has accomplished this salvation (cf. **Rev. 5:11–12; 12:10; 18:20; Jer. 51:10**).

MARRIAGE FEAST OF THE LAMB (Objective 3)
Reflect with your students on the following passages that use the bridegroom and bride imagery to tell of the relationship of the Lord and His church:

a. **Is. 50:1–3** The unfaithfulness of Israel is compared to a woman forsaken by her husband.

b. **2 Cor. 11:2** Here Paul wrote of Christ as being the husband and the church as the pure virgin.

c. **Is. 54:1–3** Paul applied this passage to those who, in Christ, have been made the children of promise.

(**Gal. 4:26–28**). During the exile Israel seemed to have been forsaken by her husband, God. But in years to come she would become the mother of many nations and peoples who would come to saving faith in Christ through the Gospel.

d. **Matt. 9:15** Jesus compared Himself to a bridegroom who was physically with His bride, His people.

e. **Eph. 5:32** The relationship between husband and wife is compared to that of Christ and His church.

f. **Is. 62:5** Here God is compared to a bridegroom who rejoices over his people, the new Israel.

g. **John 3:29** John the Baptizer compared Christ to the bridegroom and the people of God to the bride.

h. **Rev. 21:9** The Lamb is compared to the bridegroom whose wife is the church.

i. **Jer. 2:31–32** Israel's unfaithfulness was compared to a bride who forgets her wedding ornaments.

Three questions conclude this section.

1. The "fine linen" represents the righteousness of the people of God bestowed on them through the sacrificial blood of the Lamb. Corporately the church is seen clothed in the dazzling whiteness of their purity given it by Christ.

2. The phrase "*given* her to wear" emphasizes that our salvation and our life in God are free gifts bestowed on us by the Spirit for the sake of the sacrificial life, suffering, death, and resurrection of the Savior, Jesus Christ.

3. The subject broached here is worthy of substantial study. Angels are creatures of God and, with humankind, worship and serve God. Indeed, they also serve humankind. In heaven we may become *like* angels, but we will not become angels.

THE VICTOR RECEIVES HIS VICTORY (Objective 4)

1. In both passages the heavens opened—an indication that they were to receive revelations from God Himself.

2. The rider on the white horse is Christ, who is the Word of God and truth itself (cf. **John 1:1–5, 9–14**). Therefore we can fully and safely entrust to Him our whole being and future. The whiteness of the horse indicates the purity of our Lord, a purity He would also bestow in all His followers. Also, Christ will judge in purity and righteousness all those who rejected His gracious offer of salvation and life.

3. Jesus will come to judge in righteousness and justice all those who in this lifetime rejected His grace, forgiveness, and life. A person can be judged either in justice or by God's grace in Christ. If we rely on justice, we will surely be condemned eternally because of our sin. If by the power and wisdom of the Holy Spirit we are led by Him to rely on God's grace, then we are assured of eternal life.

4. No one will be able to hide from this final judgment. Christ knows the hearts of all people, and He will judge righteously and with omniscience.

5. The blood is that of Christ's enemies whom He has vanquished.

6. Christ is God's own Word revealed to humanity. To know Christ is to know God.

7. The sword is the Word of God. The Law condemns us of our sin. If we persist in living under the Law, we will perish because no human being can fulfill it. The Gospel reveals to us our Savior, and through it the Holy Spirit implants saving faith within us, sustains us in this faith, empowers us for holy living, and leads us safely amid all the temptations and troubles of this life to our eternal home.

Encourage students to look up the passages in the remaining portion of this session, and to discuss the meaning of **Revelation 19** for their personal lives of faith.

ASSIGNMENT

Suggested assignment:

1. Before the next session read **Revelation 20**.

2. Continue your study of millennialism, premillennialism, amillennialism, and postmillennialism in appropriate reference books.

42. The Millennium

BIBLE BASIS
Rev. 20:1–15

CENTRAL TRUTH

Although numerous millennial theories concerning the last times have been concocted over the years, Scripture clearly teaches that God will permit unbelief and evil to flourish in this world along with the faithful witness of God's people until Christ will return to inaugurate the New Age for His followers.

OBJECTIVES

That the students by the power of the Spirit will

1. describe the classical Christian understanding of **Revelation 20**;
2. explain why they can be confident of eventual victory in spite of the growing opposition and hostility of Christ's enemies;
3. identify the grace of God in Christ as being the foundation for their confidence and trust in their eternal salvation; and
4. describe the various millennial theories and explain in what ways they are contrary to Scripture.

INTRODUCTION

Paraphrase this paragraph from the Student Book as your introduction.

THE MILLENNIUM (Objective 1)

Have students look up the passages that are listed as references. Two questions then conclude this portion.

1. The people of God can find great hope in the words of the passages listed in the Student Book.

2. The binding of Satan began with the coming of Jesus of Nazareth into the world. The following New Testament passages describe the ongoing conflict between Jesus and Satan.

a. Jesus was led by the spirit into the wilderness to be tempted by the devil, but He resisted Him **(Matt. 4:1–11; Luke 4:1–13).**

b. Jesus cast out demons, but He would not let the demons speak because they knew who He was. The teachers of the Law accused Jesus of using the devils power to cast out these evil forces **(Mark 1:34; 3:20–30).**

c. Jesus healed a man possessed by a legion of demons by casting the demons into a herd of swine **(Mark 5:1–20).**

d. One time the demon in a possessed man cried out identifying Jesus as the "Holy One of God." Then Jesus healed the man and the evil spirit caused the man to shake and then came out of him with a shriek **(Mark 1:21–28).**

e. Though the prince of the world seemed to have triumphed with the death of Jesus on the cross, the death of Jesus was really the devil's defeat **(John 12:30–33).**

3. The second death is eternal condemnation in hell.

4. The first resurrection is a person's conversion from the death of sin in which we are born to life with God in Christ through faith. The second resurrection is the raising of our bodies at the Last Day to be reunited with our souls.

The purpose of the millennium, the New Testament age from the ascension of Christ to His Second Coming, is to enable Christians to proclaim the Gospel to all humankind.

SATAN'S DOOM (Objective 2)

Present the material in the Student Book to your class. Allow ample time for discussion. As for all sections, have students look up as many of the passages as time allows.

THE GREAT JUDGMENT (Objective 3)

Lead students through this section. Emphasize that God's criterion by which He will judge all people is His grace in Christ. All those who in this lifetime by the Spirit's power were led to saving faith already live in eternal life with God. Those who rejected God's grace in favor of living according to what they consider to be justice will be condemned.

MILLENNIAL THEORIES (Objective 4)

Take time to explain the other theories about the millennium. Have students look up the Bible passages.

Then review those passages that speak clearly of the Second Coming of Christ and their meanings for Christians.

1. In spite of our sin and unworthiness, our substitute, Jesus Christ, perfectly fulfilled God's Law in our behalf and endured the divine punishment on our sin. Therefore we face the Second Coming with the assurance that we are the people of God and heirs of heaven **(Rom. 5:9; Gal. 4:4–5; 2 Tim. 1:10; Heb. 2:14).**

2. God has placed us in this world to care for it, seek its peace and prosperity, and, above all, witness to God's saving work in Jesus Christ **(Gen. 1:28–29; 2:15; Acts 1:6–8; Eph. 4:17–6:20; 1 Tim. 6:17–19; 1 Peter 2:9).**

3. Upon our death we are with the Lord **(Phil. 1:21–26; 2 Tim. 4:6–8).**

4. Christ's Second Coming will occur at the end of this age. He then will raise our bodies in glorified form to be reunited with our souls to live before God forever **(John 6:40, 54; 1 Cor. 15:35–57; 1 Thess. 4:13–18).**

5. We can face the final judgment with joy and confidence because we will be judged not on our own merits or works, but according to the Gospel of our Savior in whom we commit our lives **(Matt. 10:31–33; Rom. 1:16–17; 2:16).**

6. Christ's Second Coming will be sudden and unexpected; therefore all predictions of the time of His coming are futile **(Matt. 24:36, 42; Mark 13:32; Luke 12:40; 1 Cor. 15:52).**

7. Rather then envision a millennium of peace and prosperity prior to the Second Coming, Scripture clearly and unequivocally affirms that evil and unbelief will abound in this world to the very end **(Matt. 24:3–14; Mark 13:3–27; Luke 21:5–28; 2 Peter 3:3–10).** Passages to which millennialists appeal for their views **(Is. 2:2–4; 11:6–9; Joel 2:23–3:21; Micah 4:14; Zech. 9:9–10; Revelation 20)** speak rather of the spiritual glory of the New Testament church which emerged with the birth of Christ and the proclamation of the Gospel in the world.

8. Only one passage, **1 Thess. 4:13–17,** speaks unequivocally of the rapture. In this passage Paul's point is that at the Second Coming those who are then living will not have an advantage over those "who have fallen asleep."

9. **Rom. 11:25–26** does not teach that all Jews eventually will be saved even as it does not affirm the universal salvation of Gentiles. In **Rom. 9:6–8,** Paul specifically states that all Israel are not the physical descendants of Abraham, but are all those who with Abraham place their trust in the promises of God as centered in Jesus Christ.

ASSIGNMENT

For your students.
1. Read **Rev. 21:1–22:21** before the next session.
2. Review the material in the Student Book for all of Revelation studied thus far.

43. The New Jerusalem

BIBLE BASIS
Rev. 21:1–22:21

CENTRAL TRUTH

By God's grace, all who acknowledge their inability to save themselves and, by the Spirit's power, place their only hope for salvation in Jesus Christ and His saving work, will reign forever with Christ in the New Age, which He will inaugurate at the Last Day.

OBJECTIVES

That the students by the power of the Spirit will

1. acknowledge that perfect peace, prosperity, and security will be established only in the world that is to come after the Last Day;
2. describe the similarities between the first Paradise **(Genesis 1–3)** and the Paradise which is to come **(Revelation 21–22)**;
3. describe the spiritual picture of the new heaven and the new earth as depicted in **Revelation 21**;
4. describe the new Jerusalem as portrayed in **Revelation 22**; and
5. express an understanding of how they are to prepare for the final consummation of this age.

INTRODUCTION (Objectives 1–2)

Use the material in the Student Book to introduce this session.

1. **Gen. 1:1/Rev. 21:1**—God created the heavens and the earth/God will establish a new heaven and a new earth.
2. **Gen. 1:14–19/Rev. 21:23–25; 22:5**—God created light/in the new heaven and earth there will be no need for created light.
3. **Gen. 3:1/Rev. 21:8**—Satan is cunning and succeeds/Satan is destroyed.
4. **Gen. 3:8/Rev. 21:3**—Humankind is alienated from God and flees from Him/humankind is redeemed and lives in closest fellowship with God.
5. **Gen. 3:22/Rev. 22:14**—People are forbidden to eat of the tree of life/people now eat freely of the tree of life.
6. **Gen. 3:22–24/Rev. 22:2**—Paradise is lost/Paradise is regained.

A NEW HEAVEN AND A NEW EARTH (Objective 3)

1. This present universe is decaying and passing away. Note the different ways in which the cited passages describe this impermanence.
2. The fire by which this world will be consumed seems to be purifying fire. This indicates this physical universe, which is God's creation, will be refined and restored to what God intended it to be. The fire of **Rev. 20:9** will eternally destroy Satan. Here fire is used in its painful, destructive sense.
3. The new heaven and new earth that John saw fulfilled in the New Age **(Rev. 21:1)** had been promised by God not only through the apostle Peter but also centuries before Christ through the prophet Isaiah.
4. "Coming down out of heaven" describes how God Himself takes the initiative to reestablish the close relationship that existed between God and man in the Garden of Eden. In the new heaven and earth this intimate relationship between God and His people will continue forever.
5. The passages cited equate Jerusalem with the people of God.
6. All of these passages speak of God's promises to establish a new Jerusalem, or a New Age, in which God will be intimately present with His people and to give them only perfect joy, peace, and contentment. In this New Age all sorrow and death will be no more.

Already in this life, as we reflect on the words and promises of God, the Holy Spirit gives us inner peace and contentment. Students can give examples of times they felt especially close to God.

7. Our whole universe will be made entirely new. In this new heaven and earth, only perfect righteousness and peace will exist. This new universe is given to us to enjoy forever without price—it is the free gift of God's grace in Jesus Christ, our Savior, who is the water of life. The sin that condemns is to reject Jesus, the water of life.

THE HOLY CITY (Objective 4)

Lead the students through this section. Invite them to look up the Bible references. Discuss any questions or observations they have.

JESUS IS COMING! (Objective 5)

Have students look up the Bible references and respond to the questions in their own way. The responses below are only examples of what might be expected.

1. What John had revealed to him is reality. We reject this to our own eternal destruction.
2. Angels are fellow servants of God with us. However, they serve perfectly while we serve imperfectly.
3. Jesus will return soon and suddenly, when we may least expect Him. In a real sense, He comes at

the time of our physical death. Many people die with no advance warning. We are always to be prepared for Him when He comes to take us **(Matt. 24:36–25:13).**

4. We are assured Jesus will come soon to take us into eternal blessedness.

5. All those who reject Christ and serve evil and Satan will be cast into eternal separation from God and everything that is good.

6. It is the Spirit of God who gives us the water of life and the power of God's grace in Christ that enables us to persist in our relationship with God until Christ comes again to receive us to be with Him forever.

ASSIGNMENT

Ask students to review all of the material in the unit on **Revelation.** For this activity you may wish to have them prepare the review material in the Student Book.

44–45. The Revelation of St. John Review and Test

These questions are to be used in Session 44 to enable students to review the material in this unit. We suggest that they complete this material in advance of the class session, and that their answers be discussed in class. You may then duplicate as many of these questions as you wish to use as a test during Session 45. Answers are included below, but you and your students may discover other valid answers in your study of Scripture.

REVELATION 1

1. What is the theme and purpose of **Revelation** (cf. **Rev. 1:1–3; 2:10; 22:20)?** A divine revelation of what is soon to occur in the history of the world as it will affect the church. To prepare Christians for what will come, they are encouraged to remain steadfast in their faith and in their mission of witnessing to the Gospel in spite of coming opposition and hostility.

Revelation also explains why this opposition and hostility should occur, why Christians must suffer, and why the future new heaven and new earth will more than compensate Christians for their suffering in this evil world. Have students draw the answer from the given passages.

2. Who are the seven spirits of God **(Rev. 1:4; cf. Ex. 25:31–40; Is. 11:1–3; Zech. 4:1–6; 1 Cor. 12:4–11; Gal. 5:22–23)?** The Holy Spirit. Seven often is used as the number of the Spirit because of the sevenfold gifts He bestows on His people **(Is. 11:1–3).**

3. In what ways does **Rev. 1:4–5** refer to each of the persons of the triune God (cf. **1 Peter 1:1–2)?** The Father is **"Him who is, and who was, and who is to come."** The Son is **"Jesus Christ, who is the faithful witness, the firstborn from the dead, and the rules of the kings of the earth."** The Holy Spirit is **"the seven spirits before His throne."**

4. To what time and event does **Rev. 1:7** refer (cf. **Matt. 24:29–35; Mark 13:24–26)?** The Last Day.

5. What does the phrase "Alpha and Omega" mean? What would be the English equivalent **(Rev. 1:8; cf. 21:6; 22:13)?** The beginning and the end. All existence is summed up in Jesus Christ, who is the eternal God. He is all in all.

6. Who is the great person in the vision whom John sees in **Rev. 1:9–20,** especially **verses 17–18** (cf. **Matt. 17:1–13)?** What does he tell John to do **(Rev. 1:1–3, 9–11, 19)?** He is Jesus Christ, who tells John to write down that which is to be revealed to him.

7. To what day of the week does the "Lord's Day" in **Rev. 1:10** refer (cf. **John 20:1, 19, 26; Acts 20:7; 1 Cor. 16:2)?** Sunday.

8. In the vision of the great person in **Rev. 1:12–16,** what is meant by the description of his dress in verses 13–15 (cf. **Dan. 7:9–22; 10:5–6)?** The robe and girdle are the clothing of the high priest and point to Christ's priestly office (cf. **Ex. 28:4; 39:29).** The white hair is the mark of the Ancient of Days **(Dan. 7:9).** The bronze feet remind us of the cherubim in Ezekiel **(Ezek. 1:7),** and the voice is that of returning glory **(Ezek. 43:2).**

REVELATION 2–3

In seven personal messages in these two chapters Jesus Christ points out things that endanger our faith and witness, making it difficult for us to hear His message in **Revelation.** To prepare us to hear and understand the message and apply it to our lives, we first must repent of the things He points out to us in these seven letters.

1. What does our Lord say to us today through His message to the Christians of Ephesus **(Rev. 2:1–7; cf. 1 Tim. 5:11–13)?** He would warn against dead orthodoxy and a loveless spirit in our commitment to the truth.

2. What would the Lord Christ say to us today through His message to the congregation of Smyrna **(2:8–11;** cf. **Heb. 12:4–13; 1 Peter 3:13–14)?** To remain faithful to Christ even unto death.

3. What is the main point of the message to the Christians of Pergamum **(2:12–17;** cf. **Numbers 22; Matt. 6:24–25, 31–33; Acts 5:11; 2 Peter 2:12–16)?** We cannot worship God and mammon. Christians are not to compromise their faith in order to get along in the world. Moreover, they are not to sin purposely in the mistaken idea that since we live in the grace of God in Christ, we are free to sin as much as we want.

4. What important message for us living today do we have in Rev. 2:18–29 (cf. **1 Kings 11:1–8; 16:31; 18:1–4**)? That Christians are not to go with the flow. We are to be faithful and honest in our Christian profession in spite of the reaction we may get from the world. We are not to do things because everyone else is doing it.

5. What does the Lord warn us against and point out to us as a failing in **Rev. 3:1–6** (cf. **Gal. 2:15–21; Eph. 2:8–9**)? Spiritual boredom—we can become so used to being Christian that it no longer means anything to us.

6. What does God point out to us in His message to the Christians of Philadelphia (**Rev. 3:7–13**; cf. **1 Cor. 16:8–9; 2 Cor. 2:12; Col. 4:3**)? We may be exemplary in our faithful adherence to the Gospel and in our commitment to Jesus Christ, but be lax in sharing our faith with others. We are not only to adhere to the pure Gospel, but we also are to share it.

7. Against what sin does Jesus warn us in **Rev. 3:14–22** (cf. **Job 33:9; Luke 18:11**)? To permit trust in one's affluence and in material possessions to lead us away from trust in God and His gifts in Christ.

8. How does Jesus identify Himself at the beginning of each of these seven letters to the churches **(Rev. 2:1; 2:8; 2:12; 2:18; 3:1; 3:7; 3:14)**?

Rev. 2:1—The One who holds the seven stars in His hand and walks among the seven golden lampstands.

Rev. 2:8—Jesus is "the First and the Last," the everliving One who is all in all. He is the One who died and rose again for our eternal salvation and life.

Rev. 2:12—He "has the sharp, double-edged sword."

Rev. 2:18—Jesus has eyes "like blazing fire," and His "feet are like burnished bronze."

Rev. 3:1—Jesus is He who sends the sevenfold Spirit of God and has the seven stars.

Rev. 3:7—Jesus is He who is holy and true, and who holds the key of David.

Rev. 3:14—Jesus is "the faithful and true witness, the ruler of God's creation."

9. With what blessing of promise does each of the letters end **(Rev. 2:7; 2:11; 2:17; 2:26–29; 3:5; 3:12; 3:21)**?

Rev. 2:7—Jesus promises the Spirit to give them victory over their lovelessness and to bestow on them eternal life.

Rev. 2:10—God will give a crown of life to those who remain faithful to death.

Rev. 2:17—He will at the Last Day give His own "hidden manna" (the fulness of Christ), and a "white stone" (holiness, beauty, and glory that will endure forever).

Rev. 2:26–29—To those who remain faithful God will give the privilege of ruling with Him throughout all eternity, sharing with Christ His royal splendor and dominion.

Rev. 3:5—Those who remain spiritually alive will inherit eternal life.

Rev. 3:12—Jesus promises to keep His people safe in the time of trial, and He promises those who endure will be pillars in the temple of heaven, where they will dwell securely forever.

Rev. 3:21—Whatever affliction God's people may endure will be for their eternal good.

REVELATION 4–5

In **Revelation 4–5** we have the inaugural vision of heaven to introduce the prophecy and message of the Book of Revelation.

1. Who is the person sitting on the throne (**Rev. 4:2–3**; cf. **Is. 6:1–3; Ezek. 1:26–28; Rev. 4:8–11**)? The heavenly Father, the Lord of all things.

2. Whom do the 24 elders represent in **Rev. 4:4** (cf. **Ex. 3:16; Matt. 19:27–28; Rev. 21:12–14**)? The people of God from the beginning of time to the Last Day—the 24 represent the 12 tribes of Israel (the people of God throughout the OT period), and the 12 apostles (the people of God of the entire NT era).

3. Who are the four beasts (or creatures) with the different faces in **Rev. 4:6–8** (cf. **Is. 6:1–3; Ezek. 1:1–28; 10:8–22**)? The cherubim, a higher order of angels who are in the forefront of the hosts of angels worshiping God. Eyes—alertness and knowledge; lion—service to God and humankind with courage and strength; ox—patient steadfastness and strength in their service; human face—intelligence and wisdom; eagle—eagerness and swiftness to serve.

4. What does the book or scroll with the seven seals which is given to the conquering Lamb represent (**Rev. 5:1–5**; cf. **Is. 29:11–19; Ezek. 2:1–10**)? The contents of the revelation that John is to receive and to communicate to the people of God on earth.

5. Who is the Lamb in **Rev. 5:6** (cf. **Is. 53:5–7; John 1:29; 1 Peter 1:18–19; Rev. 5:12**)? Jesus Christ, the world's Redeemer, the Lion of the tribe of Judah.

6. What is the significance of the seven eyes and seven horns on the Lamb (**Rev. 5:6**; cf. **Deut. 33:17; Zech. 4:10; Rev. 1:4; 4:5**)? This imagery depicts the mission of Christ in the world through the activity of the Holy Spirit. The seven eyes refer to the complete knowledge and wisdom to be found in Christ, and the seven horns refer to His complete strength and power. Thus Christ through the Holy Spirit endows His witnesses on earth with strength, power, wisdom, and knowledge for the fulfillment of their mission.

7. What might the action of the receiving of the scroll by the Lamb mean (**Rev. 5:6–10**; cf. **Dan. 7:9–14; Matt. 26:64; John 5:22**)? This action represents Christ's enthronement at the ascension to reign with the Father as Lord of lords. Because of His sacrificial life, death, and resurrection, Christ is the Mediator through whom alone we can approach the throne of God.

8. Why would all the heavenly court (hosts) wor-

ship the Lamb (**Rev. 5:8–14**; cf. **John 5:22–23**)? He is the only Savior through whom we can approach the Father. Therefore He is worthy of the worship given to God. Indeed, we humans cannot approach God except through the mediating role of Jesus.

REVELATION 6–8

In these three chapters we have a preview of things that are to come to pass from the time of Jesus' death and ascension to the end of this age. This **(Rev. 6:1–7:17)** is the first of three cyclic views. **Chapter 8** forms an interlude during which we are given a sweeping view of things to come, and which introduces the second cycle.

1. What does each of the four horsemen represent (**Rev. 6:1–8**; cf. **Zech. 1:7–21; 6:1–8**)? The white horseman—suffering people undergo because of human lust for power and tyranny over other people. Red horse—conflict, war, bloodshed. Black horse—famine, poverty, economic imbalance. Pale horse—disease and death.

2. Give at least two examples from today's world for each of the four horsemen. A variety of answers are possible.

3. The fifth seal when opened in **verses 9–11** of **chapter 6** gives us a picture of God's saints. What is the connection between the picture of the saints given with the opening of the fifth seal **(Rev. 6:9–11)**, and that of the four horsemen of the first four seals (**Rev. 6:1–8**; cf. **Acts 14:21–22**)? Although Christians are not *of* the world, they yet are *in* the world and must also suffer with all humanity the consequences of sin as depicted by the four horsemen. Indeed, at times they are called upon to suffer just because they are followers of Christ; for example, the white horseman in his tyranny may demand the absolute devotion of people and will not tolerate the worship of God.

4. What does the sixth seal represent (**Rev. 6:12–17**; cf. **Joel 2:28–32; Matt. 24:29–31; Luke 21:5–6; 2 Peter 3:11–13**)? The end of the world which will be preceded by a wide variety of catastrophes in the natural universe.

5. Who are the 144,000 of **Rev. 7:1–8** (cf. **Rev. 14:1–3**)? All of the people of God from the beginning of the world to the end who have been kept secure in the faith by the Holy Spirit during their sojourn in the world, and who now are before the throne of the Lamb for all eternity.

6. Who are those dressed in white robes in heaven (**Rev. 7:9–17**; cf. **Rev. 3:5, 18; 4:4; 6:11; 7:13–14; 19:14**)? The people of God whose robes have been washed in the blood of the Lamb. We enter heaven not because of our merits and accomplishments, but solely because of the saving life and work of Jesus Christ, the Savior.

7. The opening of the seventh seal introduces a second sweeping view of things that will happen from the time of Christ up to the end. What is the difference between the view of things to happen introduced by the six seals in **Rev. 6:1–7:17**, and the view introduced by the trumpet blasts in **Rev. 8:1–13** (cf. **Ex. 9:23–25; Luke 21:9–11**)? The view of **Rev. 6:1–7:17** focuses on the evils and tribulations people experience because of human sin—man's inhumanity to man. This view emphasizes evils in human relationships. The second cycle of the seven trumpets focus on the evils in nature caused by sin and that result in human suffering.

REVELATION 9–11

Revelation 9–11 continues the second cyclic view of all things from the time of Christ up to the end. The four trumpet blasts in **Rev. 8:1–13** introduce this view.

1. Who is the star falling from heaven, the leader of the locusts, called Abaddon, the angel in charge of the Abyss (Rev. 9:1; cf. **Is. 14:11–12; Luke 10:18; Rev. 12:9**)? Who are the locusts? Satan. The locusts are his supernatural followers, the demons.

2. What warning are we to derive from this picture of the locusts and their leader assaulting humankind (**Rev. 9:1–11**; cf. **Job 1:6–12; 2:7; Luke 9:42; 1 Peter 5:8–9**)? We need to be aware that a supernatural world of devils are constantly assaulting us to lead us away from God and eternal life. By the power of the Spirit through the Word, we must continuously defend ourselves against these attacks.

3. Why is it that after all the judgments that God brings on mankind because of sin, people don't repent? (**Rev. 9:20–21**; cf. **Dan. 3:1–30**)? A variety of answers can be given. One cause is that Satan has so darkened the minds of people that they can't perceive truth when it's before them. Another reason is that they are so enamored with their gods of this world, such as material possessions, sensual pleasures, and popularity, that they want to cling to these gods in spite of all afflictions.

4. In **chapter 10** and in the first 13 verses of **chapter 11** there is an interlude between the sixth and seventh trumpet blasts. What is the message of God to us in the interlude between the sixth and seventh trumpet blasts (**Rev. 10:1–13:13**, esp. **10:11** and **11:3–11**)? God in His grace and mercy is delaying the seventh blast which will bring the world to an end. During this time we Christians are to be busy sharing the saving Gospel of Jesus Christ with all people so that they may escape the righteous judgment of God to come, and thus be saved eternally.

5. What do the temple and the two witnesses represent in **Rev. 11:1–13** (cf. **Deut. 19:15; Zech. 4:3, 11–14; Eph. 2:20–22; 1 Cor. 3:16; 2 Cor. 6:16**)? All believers. They will be protected by God as they seek to fulfill their mission even as He permits evils to befall unbelievers in punishment for their sin.

REVELATION 12

Together with **Rev. 20:1–10** this chapter is the key to understanding **Revelation.**

1. Whom does the woman represent (**Rev. 12:1–2**; cf. **Micah 4:9–10; Luke 2:1–7**)? What is the significance of her clothing? The church, or people of God as typified by the Virgin Mary, from whom the Savior was born. Her garment of the sun denotes glory and exaltation. The moon suggests dominance. The wreath of 12 stars suggests victory and royalty (12 is a number for the church.) This is a description of the church on earth as seen from heaven.

2. Who is the child born to the woman? (**Rev. 12:2, 5**; cf. **Ps. 2:6–9; Luke 2:1–7**)? Jesus Christ, the promised Messiah and Savior.

3. Who is the dragon (**Rev. 12:3–5, 9**; cf. **Gen. 3:1–16; Matt. 2:13–19; Rev. 20:2**)? Satan.

4. What is the significance of the archangel Michael (**Rev. 12:7**; cf. **Dan. 10:13, 21; 12:1; Jude 9**)? Michael is the guardian of Israel who protects the people of God from Satan and his wily temptations and assaults. He intercedes for God's people (**Jude 9**), fights their enemies, and leads them safely into heaven.

5. When did this war, in which Michael cast the devil out of heaven, take place (**Rev. 12:7–12; Is. 14:11 ff.; Job 1:8 ff.; Zech. 3:1 ff.; Luke 10:17–19; John 12:27–33**)? When Satan in his desire to usurp his Creator's position and power was expelled from heaven at the victory of Christ's death, resurrection, and ascension.

6. After being cast from heaven, the dragon persecutes the woman. What is the significance of the two wings of an eagle (**Rev. 12:13–14**; cf. **Ex. 19:4–5**)? Even as God bore the Israelites on the wings of eagles from the tyranny of Egypt to the wilderness of safety from Pharaoh's forces, so God bears His people from the clutches of Satan into the wilderness—a haven of safety. **Rev. 12:13–14** needs to be compared with **Ex. 19:4–5** so that the connection can be made.

REV. 13:1–14:5

1. What forces or powers does the beast from the sea represent (**Rev. 13:1–10**; cf. **Daniel 7**)? All tyrannical powers in any field of human endeavor, but especially in the political sphere.

2) What does the beast from the earth in **Rev. 13:11–18** (cf. **Matt. 7:15; 2 Thess. 2:1–12; Rev. 17:1–3**) represent? All religions and philosophies opposed to the Gospel of Jesus Christ.

3. What is the significance of the seven heads and ten horns which the dragon shares with the beast (**Rev. 12:3; 13:1; 17:1–3**)? The seven heads of the beast emphasizes its relationship to the dragon, who also has seven heads. First-century readers probably saw in the seven heads an allusion to tyrannical Rome with its seven hills. The ten horns represent power—absolute power, and the brute force by which tyrannical governments use to gain their mastery over the bodies and souls of people.

4. What does the beast from the earth having two horns like a lamb but speaking like a dragon signify (**Rev. 13:11**; cf. **Matt. 7:15; 24:11, 23–24**)? This beast appears to be harmless and even is similar to Christ. He promises deliverance from human woes and ultimate good to all who listen to him. But his message is that of Satan. This beast is all religions and philosophies that would lead people away from the justification by grace through faith that Christ offers to trust in human thinking for ultimate good.

5. What does the number *666* mean (**Rev. 13:18**)? Six is the number of man and probably refers to the unholy trinity of Satan and the two beasts by which the church is assaulted. It also points to the failures of human governments throughout history to resolve the problems and consequences of sin. This solution lies only in the grace of God through Christ Jesus.

6. Who are the 144,000 (**Rev. 14:1–5**; cf. **Ps. 33:1–5; 40:1–4; 96:1–13; 98:1–3; Rev. 3:12; 7:1–8**)? What do their songs and actions symbolize? These are all of the believers throughout all human history. This number equals all of the Old Testament believers as represented by the 12 tribes of Israel, times the New Testament believers represented by the 12 apostles, times 1,000, the number that points to ultimate completeness and perfection. Their song reflects their joy and gratitude in enjoying the glories of heaven because of the salvation God gained for them in the substitutionary life, death, and resurrection of the Savior, Jesus Christ.

7. What does the statement that the 144,000 are pure and have not had relations with women mean (**Rev. 14:4**; cf. **2 Cor. 11:2; Eph. 5:25–27**)? By the power of the Spirit through the Word the saints persevered in their trust in Jesus Christ and His redeeming, cleansing blood as they fought for their Lord.

REV. 14:6–16:21

1. What is the meaning of Babylon (**Rev. 14:8**; cf. **Rev. 16:19; 17:2–5; 18:1–3**)? In John's day Babylon was probably Rome and its empire. It was a code word for luxurious, sumptuous living without regard to the divine will or to human welfare. In the course of history many "Babylons" have arisen and fallen. Our late 20th century American civilization is in danger of becoming a Babylon.

2. Upon whom do the three angels pronounce judgment in **Rev. 14:6–12**? Upon those who place their ultimate trust for their good in things of this world, especially in the political powers. Other such gods who can tyrannize the minds and souls of people can include tyrannical, dominating leaders in business, industry, science, education, and other fields of human endeavor. For example, at times college students are called upon to deny their faith in order to succeed academically.

3. What encouragement and assurance do you find in **Rev. 14:13** (cf. **1 Cor. 15:54–58; Heb. 4:10–11**)? This is an encouragement to remain faithful in

spite of the opposition and hostility of Satan and his minions. Our eternal goal is well worth any price we need to pay in this world for faithfulness. In heaven we no longer will need to strive against evil and Satan.

4. What event is represented by the picture of the harvest of the earth (**Rev. 14:14–20**; cf. **Matt. 13:24–30, 36–43**)? Judgment day.

5. Why are the plagues of **Rev. 15:1** called the last plagues of God? These are the final plagues to assail humankind immediately before the Second Coming of Christ.

6. What is meant by Armageddon in **Rev. 16:16** (cf. **Mark 13:14–27; Rev. 20:7–10**)? Is there such a geographical place (**Judg. 5:19–20; 1 Kings 18:16–40; 2 Kings 23:29; 2 Chron. 35:22–23**)? Armageddon is the final, all-out effort of Satan and the political, philosophical, religious powers he controls to destroy the church. Possibly Armageddon is a reference to Megiddo near which the Israelites under Deborah overcame their enemies, where Elijah confronted the prophets of Baal, and the godly king Josiah met his untimely death at the hands of the enemies of the Lord.

REVELATION 17–19

1. Who is the "great prostitute" (**Revelation 17**; cf. **Mark 13:14–23; 2 Thess. 2:1–12; 1 John 4:1–6; Revelation 13**)? How do the seven heads and the ten horns of the scarlet beast (**Rev. 17:3**) help us to identify her (cf. **Rev. 12:3; 13:1; 17:9–12**)? The great prostitute would be all those seductive powers that seduce people, especially Christians, to forsake God and to follow Satan. All philosophies and religions that direct us to place our trust in ourselves and in human institutions rather than in the free, justifying grace of God for the sake of the life, suffering, death, and resurrection of Jesus Christ would be such a harlot. False Christianity and political powers, symbolized by the seven heads and ten horns would also be such powers. Such was Rome in John's day and the Roman papacy in Luther's time. In the recent past we have had political powers such as Nazi Germany and Stalinist Russia who have sorely oppressed Christians in their desire for the mastery of human minds and souls.

2. Why do you think John marveled at the great harlot (**Rev. 17:6; 18:9–24**)? One reason for John's astonishment would be the power over the eternal lives of people that such a destructive monster could wield.

3. Can we identify the Babylon that is spoken of in **chapter 18** (cf. **Rev. 13:1–18; 14:8; 17:2–5**)? Why? The description given the Babylon can readily be applied to various religious, philosophical, and political powers that have emerged throughout history. In John's day Rome was such a Babylon. Today not only certain political powers, but also powers in religion, education, and other areas of human endeavor try to negate Jesus Christ as he reveals Himself to us in Scripture.

4. Who is the bride of the Lamb in the marriage feast in heaven (**Rev. 19:7–9**; cf. **Matt. 22:1–14**)? The people of God, the church.

5. Who is the rider on the white horse (**Rev. 19:11**)? Who is the Word of God (**19:13**; cf. **John 1:1–2, 14; Rev. 1:12–16, especially v. 16**)? Jesus Christ.

6. Why is His robe covered in blood (**Rev. 19:13**; cf. **Is. 63:1–3; Rev. 14:14–20**)? Normally we would expect the blood to refer to that which Christ shed for the sin of all humankind. However, here it is the blood of judgment—the blood of all those who opposed Him who now must endure the result of the decisions and actions they themselves made.

REVELATION 20–22

1. What does the period of one thousand years (millennium) symbolize (**Rev. 20:1–3**; cf. **Rev. 11:1–13; 12:7–12**)? The complete (1,000 is the number for completeness) New Testament period of the preaching of God's grace in Christ from His life, death, and ascension to the Last Day.

2. When was Satan bound (**Mark 3:20–27; Luke 10:17–18; John 12:31–33; 2 Peter 2:4; Jude 6**)? This binding occurred with the liberating life, suffering, death, resurrection, and ascension of Jesus Christ. God has bound Satan so that the Gospel might be freely proclaimed. True, Satan still is able to entice, seduce, and influence human beings; but he cannot exercise tyrannical control that would prevent the proclamation of the saving Gospel.

3. What is the "first resurrection" (**Rev. 20:5**; cf. **John 5:24–27; Rom. 6:2–5; Eph. 2:1–6; Col. 2:12; 3:1**)? This is our rising from the death of sin and eternal condemnation (our original estate as human beings) to a new life as people of God. This would be regeneration, conversion, the new birth through faith.

4. What is the "second resurrection" (**Rev. 20:11–15**; cf. **Job 19:23–27; John 5:28–29; 1 Cor. 15:1–58; 1 Thess. 4:13–18**)? The resurrection of our bodies on the Last Day at the Second Coming of Christ.

5. What is meant by the "second death" (**Rev. 20:6, 14**; cf. **Rev. 2:11; 21:8**)? What would be the first death (**Rev. 20:5**; cf. **Rom. 6:2–5; Eph. 2:1–6**)? The second death is eternal separation from God in hell. The first death is our death in sin and our opposition against God, one result of which is temporal death.

6. What is meant by the "new heavens and the new earth" (**Rev. 21:1**; cf. **Is. 60:19–20; 65:17–25; 66:22; 2 Peter 3:7–13**)? At Christ's Second Coming He will restore this universe to that which God created it to be—a perfect paradise.

7. What understanding of heaven might one draw from **Rev. 22:1–5** (cf. **Genesis 2; Ezek. 47:7–12; Rom. 8:18–23**)? Heaven will be paradise regained. It will be this universe as God at creation intended it to be. There we will enjoy only perfect, eternal bliss.

8. Why is **Rev. 22:17–21** (cf. **Luke 23:46**) a fitting conclusion not only to **Revelation** but also to the entire Bible? Allow for any valid answer. For example, we are

encouraged to take the revelation God gives us through Scripture at face value, neither adding nor diminishing therefrom. We are to anticipate the future expectantly, always preparing ourselves for the Second Coming. We can face the future joyfully and confidently, knowing that the climax of our existence as Christian lies in the future when Christ will return for us.

"Amen. Come, Lord Jesus. The grace of the Lord Jesus be with God's people. Amen" **(Rev. 22:20–21)**. This is the prayer of the church as each day she seeks to fulfill her task.

www.ingramcontent.com/pod-product-compliance
Lightning Source LLC
Chambersburg PA
CBHW080456170426
43196CB00016B/2825